THE WISDOM OF GANDHI

THE WISDOM OF GANDHI

With an Introduction by

Thomas Kiernan

Philosophical Library

New York

Library of Congress Catalog Card No. 67–29203

The publisher wishes to express acknowledgment, in preparing this
little volume, to Pearl Publications Private Limited, Bombay, and to
Mr. Anand T. Hingorani, editor of *The Art of Living*.

Distributed to the Trade by

BOOK SALES INC.

352 Park Ave South

New York, N.Y., 10010

INTRODUCTION

Mohandas Karamchand Gandhi was born in India in 1869. Educated in his native land and in England, he became a lawyer in 1889. After a stay in South Africa, where he fought for the rights of Indians in that country, he returned to India in 1915 and began working for its independence. He gave up his acquired Western way of life to live a life of abstinence in accordance with Hindu ethics and very quickly became a popular leader. He served several times as leader of the Indian National Congress and became celebrated throughout the world for his practice of the policy of non-violent resistance to British rule. He was jailed on several occasions by British authorities, but this treatment only served to stiffen his resistance to India's status as an English colony. He was the moving force in conferences that finally led to India's independence in 1947, but was deeply disappointed by India's partition. He was assassinated on January 30, 1948, by a Hindu who blamed him for the partition.

Gandhi, very early in his political life, became known as Mahatma (the great souled) and, as a political figure, was unique in the history of the modern world. Not only was he a selfless servant of his people, he was also a thinker of simple but great profundity. His political philosophy viewed service as the highest end of life and considered the good of others as intimately bound up with one's own good. On the basis of this vision Gandhi set out a vital and compelling blueprint for the highest form of living and endeavored, with much success, to follow it. The example he set became an inspiration for many people and had no small impact on political philosophy.

CONTENTS

THE WISDOM OF GANDHI

CHAPTER I

ON MORALITY AND MAN'S DUTY

The Moral Law

PEOPLE in the West generally hold that the whole duty of man is to promote the happiness of the majority of mankind, and happiness is supposed to mean only physical happiness and economic prosperity. If the laws of morality are broken in the conquest of this happiness, it does not matter very much. Again, as the object sought to be attained is the happiness of the majority, Westerners do not think there is any harm if this is secured by sacrificing a minority. The consequences of this line of thinking are writ large on the face of Europe.*

This exclusive search for physical and economic well-being prosecuted in disregard of morality is contrary to Divine Law, as some wise men in the West have shown. One of these was John Ruskin, who contends in **Unto This Last** that men can be happy only if they obey the Moral Law.

We, in India, are very much given nowadays to an imitation of the West. It is necessary to imitate the virtues of the West, but there is no doubt that Western standards are often bad, and everyone will agree that we should shun all evil things.

Morality is an essential ingredient in all the faiths of the world ; but, apart from religion, our commonsense indicates the necessity of observing the Moral Law. Only by observing it can we hope to be happy.[1]

---

* "I do not believe in the doctrine of the greatest good of the greatest number. It means, in its nakedness, that in order to achieve the supposed good of 51 per cent, the interest of 49 per cent may be, or rather, should be sacrificed. It is a heartless doctrine and has done harm to humanity. The only real, dignified, human doctrine is the greatest good of all, and this can only be achieved by uttermost self-sacrifice."

—*M. D.'s Diary* : p. 149.

The Duty of Looking Within

THERE are two windows to the mind of every man, the one revealing himself as he is, the other as he ought to be. It is the duty of every human being to look carefully within, and see himself as he is, and spare no pains to improve himself in body, mind and soul. He should realize the mischief wrought by injustice, wickedness, vanity, and the like, and do his best to fight them. The moral principles that are not followed in practice are good for nothing. We see many men who get by heart maxims of morality, and who talk loudly about them, but who have not the least idea of putting them in practice. There are others who think that all rules of morality are intended only for our guidance in a future world ! But we can unhesitatingly assert that he, who is not prepared to order his life in unquestioning obedience to the laws of morality, cannot be said to be a man in the full sense of the word. We should all be able to find our happiness in righteousness and veracity, in spite of the pains and losses which we may have to suffer in this world.

God is omnipotent. He is the embodiment of perfection. None can set limit to His justice and His mercy. How, then, can we, who call ourselves His devotees, dare to infringe the obligation of morality ? We should not, of course, lead a moral life in the hope of a reward. A life of goodness is enjoined upon us, not because it will bring good to us, but because it is the eternal and immutable law of Nature. Good works are, indeed, more than food and raiment to us. We should feel more grateful to one who gives us an opportunity of doing a good deed than to him who feeds us in our hunger.

No man who cares only for show, or who is anxious to make a figure in the world, can be really moral. Morality does not consist in cleanliness, or knowledge, or industry. All these, of course, are a part of morality, but by themselves they are not sufficient to make a man moral. The really moral man leads a life of virtue, not because it will do him good, but because it is the law of his being, the very breath of his nostrils. In a word, virtue is its own reward.

True Morality

TRUE morality consists not in following the beaten track, but in finding out the true path for ourselves, and in fearlessly following it. True progress is impossible without such strenuous pursuit of Truth. In other words, progress and reform are always intimately bound up with morality.

Our desires and motives may be divided into the classes — selfish and unselfish. All selfish desires are immoral, while the desire to improve ourselves for the sake of doing good to others is truly moral. But, if we begin to boast of our services to others, or even to feel proud of them, we cease to be moral men. Virtuous action consists in a strenuous pursuit of good merely for the sake of doing good.

The individual or the family that allows an entrance to the germs of immorality—anger, falsehood, dissension and the like, is ruined for ever. The power to do good does not come to us from without. It exists always within us, and we have only to develop it by proper means. The highest moral law is that we should unremittingly work for the good of mankind.

Morality and Universal Good

MAN is worse than the brute, so long as he is selfish and indifferent to the happiness of others. He rises above the level of the brute, when he begins to work for the welfare of his family. He rises higher in the scale when he comes to look upon his whole community or race as his own family. He becomes greater still when he begins to regard even the so-called barbarous races as the members of his own family. In other words, man becomes great exactly in the degree in which he works for the welfare of his fellow-men.

And so long as we do not feel sympathy and love for every one of our fellow-beings, we cannot be said to have understood the Moral Law. The highest morality is universal. We should render devoted service to the world in every possible way, remembering that every one of our brethren has a claim on us. Those who think that they are responsible only to themselves can never be men of high character. It is, of course, a silly and a dangerous notion that the man who does not safeguard his own interests must fail in the struggle for existence. God will never forsake those who devote themselves to the service of others with a purity and a singleness of aim.

Mankind is one, seeing that all are equally subject to the Moral Law. All men are equal in God's eyes. There are, of course, differences of race and status and the like ; but the higher the status of a man, the greater is his responsibility. If we happen to occupy a high position, we ought not to boast of our superiority, and look down upon those who are below us. We do our work, as they theirs. And all work towards a common end — the welfare of humanity. So long as we think otherwise, we cannot call ourselves moral men.

The Moral Law also requires that the strong men of a community or nation should regard it as their paramount duty to protect the weak and the oppressed. If all men realized the obligation of service, they would regard it as a sin to amass wealth ; and then, there would be no inequalities of wealth, and consequently no famine or starvation. Those who tread the path of virtue should not be disheartened by the thought that virtue is so rare in the world, and that they are in a minority. Their duty is simply to do the right, and leave the rest to God. They should never think of the result of their action, for the only reward of a thing well done is to have done it.

Man's Duty

MAN'S duty is to do unselfish service to others ; and he should do such service not in order to do good to others, but rather because it is the very law of his being. There are some people who think that we can afford to act as we please in matters that affect only ourselves, but no man can, in fact, do anything in the world which does not, directly or indirectly, affect the welfare of his fellow-men.

Everyone must remember that his most secret thoughts have an influence on himself as well as on others. He should, therefore, practise self-control so as to put all evil thoughts out of his mind, and give room only for thoughts that are noble and great. He should keep his body as clean and spotless as his mind. A man is but the product of his thoughts. What he thinks, that he becomes. Hence, all temptations to evil must be sternly repressed. No one who has not become the complete master of his senses and his passions, can come to any good.

The man who has learnt to keep his mind spotlessly pure, must also have a clear conception of his goal in life. The man, who starts on his career with no fixed idea of his goal, must dissipate his energies and finally be lost for ever, even as a rudderless boat is tossed hither and thither by the waves of the sea and finally destroyed. The noblest of all aims is the worship of God. And the highest form of worship consists in doing the work of God by living in obedience to the Moral Law, and by rendering disinterested service to humanity. Thousands of men who are wicked and depraved take the name of God in vain. A parrot can be taught to repeat the name of God ; but can it be called godly or pious ? Service of man is possible to all men under all circumstances. The man who regards service as the highest end of his life cannot help being highly moral ; for the welfare of the world is intimately bound up with the exercise of the moral virtues.

In judging the actions of men, we should always apply this test — whether it conduces to the welfare of the world or not. The merchant should see that he does not profit himself at the expense of his customers, lawyers and doctors should think of the interests of their clients rather than of their own earnings. The mother should always take care to see that her child is not spoilt by false affection or otherwise. A poor unlettered labourer is by far a greater man than the clever merchant, lawyer, or doctor who has earned his money by unworthy means. Let us never forget that even the meanest of us is capable of guiding his life by the above principle. Even the humblest of us can rise above the limitations of wealth and rank ; for a man's greatness rests not on wealth or social position, but simply and solely on his life and conduct. To judge the character of a man, we should know the inner workings of his heart. One man may give a rupee to a beggar in order to send him away from his sight ; while another may give him four annas moved by pity and love. Of these two, the latter is clearly the better man, although he has given much less than the former.

To sum up, then, that man alone can be called truly religious or moral whose mind is not tainted with hatred or selfishness, and who leads a life of absolute purity and of disinterested service ; and that man alone can be called truly wealthy or happy either. Only such men can do good to mankind ; for Truth is the foundation of all that is good and great. To a true servant of humanity, the question never arises as to the best form of service. When we have realized the majesty of the Moral Law, we shall see how little our happiness or unhappiness depends on health, and success, and fame, and the like. As has been finely said by Emerson, even the pains and griefs of good men contribute to their happiness, while even the wealth and fame of bad men cause misery to themselves as well as to the world.

'Seek ye first the Kingdom of God and His righteousness, and all other things shall be added unto you.'[2]

CHAPTER II

ON MATERIALISM AND MAMMON WORSHIP

'Take No Thought for the Morrow'

"TAKE no thought for the morrow' is an injunction which finds an echo in almost all the religious scriptures of the world. In well-ordered society the securing of one's livelihood should be, and is, found to be the easiest thing in the world. Indeed, the test of orderliness in a country is not the number of millionaires it owns, but the absence of starvation among its masses. The only statement that has to be examined is, whether it can be laid down as a law of universal application that material advancement means moral progress.

Now, let us take a few illustrations. Rome suffered a moral fall when it attained high material affluence. So did Egypt, and so perhaps most countries of which we have any historical record. The descendants and kinsmen of the royal and divine Krishna, too, fell when they were rolling in riches. We do not deny to the Rockefellers and the Carnegies possession of an ordinary measure of morality, but we gladly judge them indulgently. I mean that we do not even expect them to satisfy the highest standard of morality. With them, material gain has not necessarily meant moral gain.

The question we are asking ourselves is not a new one. It was addressed of Jesus two thousand years ago. St. Mark has vividly described the scene. Jesus is in his solemn mood. He is earnest. He talks of Eternity. He knows the world about him. He is himself the greatest economist of his time. He succeeded in economizing time and space ; he transcended them. It is to him at his best that one comes running, kneels down, and asks : "Good Master, what shall I do that I may inherit Eternal Life ?"

8

And Jesus said unto him : "Why callest thou me good ? There is none good but one, that is God. Thou knowest the Commandments. Do not commit adultery ; Do not kill ; Do not steal ; Do not bear false witness ; Defraud not ; Honour thy father and mother." And he answered and said unto him : "Master, all these have I observed from my youth." Then Jesus, beholding him, loved him and said unto him : "One thing thou lackest ! Go thy way, sell whatever thou hast and give to the poor, and thou shall have treasure in Heaven. Come, take up the Cross and follow me."

And he was sad at that saying and went away grieved, for he had great possession. And Jesus looked round about and said unto the disciple : "How hardly shall they that have riches enter into the Kingdom of God." And the disciples were astonished at his words. But Jesus answereth again and said unto them : "Children, how hard is it for them that trust in riches to enter into the Kingdom of God. It is easier for a camel to go through the eye of a needle than for a rich man to enter into the Kingdom of God."*

Here you have an eternal rule of life stated in the noblest words the English language is capable of producing. But the disciples nodded unbelief, as we do even to this day. To him they said, as we say today : "But, look, how the Law fails in practice. If we sell all and have nothing, we shall have nothing to eat. We must have money or we cannot even be reasonably moral." So they state their case thus :—And they were astonished out of measure, saying among themselves : "Who, then, can be saved ?" And Jesus looking upon them said : "With men it is impossible, but not with God ; for, with God all things are possible." Then, Peter began to say unto him : "Lo, we

---

* "The Kingdom of Heaven is for those who are poor in spirit. Let us, therefore, learn at every step to reduce our needs and wants to the terms of the poor and try to be truly poor in spirit."

—*Young India* : January 12, 1928.

have left all, and have followed thee." And Jesus answered and said : 'Verily, I say unto you there is no man that has left house or brethren or sisters, or father or mother or wife or children or lands for my sake and Gospel's but he shall receive one hundredfold, now in this time, houses and brethren and sisters and mothers and children and land ; and, in the world to come, Eternal Life. But many that are first shall be last and the last, first."

You have here the result or reward, if you prefer the term, of following the Law. I have not taken the trouble of copying similar passages from the other non-Hindu scriptures, and I will not insult you by quoting in support of the Law stated by Jesus, passages from the writings and sayings of our own sages, passages even stronger, if possible, than the Biblical extracts I have drawn your attention to. Perhaps, the strongest of all the testimonies in favour of the affirmative answer to the question before us are the lives of the greatest teachers of the world. Jesus, Mohammed, Buddha, Nanak, Kabir, Chaitanya, Shankara, Dayananda, Ramakrishna were men who exercised an immense influence over, and moulded the character of, thousands of men. The world is the richer for their having lived in it. And they were all men who deliberately embraced poverty as their lot.

I should not have laboured my point as I have done, if I did not believe that, in so far as we have made the modern materialistic craze our goal, so far are we going down-hill on the path of progress. I hold that economic progress, in the sense I have put it, is antagonistic to real progress. Hence, the ancient ideal has been the limitation of activities promoting wealth. This does not put an end to all material ambition. We should still have, as we have always had, in our midst people who make the pursuit of wealth their aim in life. But we have always recognized that it is a fall from the ideal. It is a beautiful thing to know that the wealthiest among us have often felt that to have remained voluntarily poor would have been a higher state for them. That you cannot serve God and Mammon is an economic truth of the highest value. We have to make our choice.

Western nations are today groaning under the heel of the Monster God of Materialism. Their moral growth has become stunted. They measure their progress in £. sh. d. American wealth has become the standard. She is the envy of the other nations. I have heard many of our countrymen say that we shall gain American wealth but avoid its methods. I venture to suggest that such an attempt, if it were made, is foredoomed to failure. We cannot be 'wise, temperate and furious' in a moment. I would have our leaders teach us to be morally supreme in the world. This land of ours was once, we are told, the abode of the Gods. It is not possible to conceive Gods inhabiting a land which is made hideous by the smoke and the din of mill-chimneys and factories, and whose roadways are traversed by rushing engines, dragging numerous cars crowded with men who know not for the most part what they are after, who are often absent-minded, and whose tempers do not improve by being uncomfortably packed like sardines in boxes ; and, finding themselves in the midst of utter strangers, who would oust them if they could and whom they would, in their turn, oust similarly. I refer to these things because they are held to be symbolical of material progress. But they add not an atom to our happiness.[1]

Multiplication of Wants

I DO not believe that multiplication of wants and machinery contrived to supply them is taking the world a single step nearer its goal. I whole-heartedly detest this mad desire to destroy distance and time, to increase animal appetites and go to the ends of the earth in search of their satisfaction. If modern civilization stands for all this, and I have understood it to do so, I call it Satanic.[2]

Civilization, in the real sense of the term, consists not in the multiplication, but in the deliberate and voluntary restriction of wants. This alone promotes real happiness and contentment, and increases the capacity for service.[3]

Search for Material Comforts

EUROPEAN civilization is no doubt suited for the Europeans, but it will mean ruin for India if we endeavour to copy it. This is not to say that we may not adopt and assimilate whatever may be good and capable of assimilation by us, as it does not also mean that even the Europeans will not have to part with whatever evil might have crept into it. The incessant search for material comforts and their multiplication is such an evil, and I make bold to say that the Europeans themselves will have to remodel their outlook, if they are not to perish under the weight of the comforts to which they are becoming slaves. It may be that my reading is wrong, but I know that for India to run after the Golden Fleece is to court certain death. Let us engrave on our hearts the motto of a Western philosopher : 'Plain living and high thinking'. Today, it is certain that the millions cannot have high living and we, the few who profess to do the thinking for the masses, run the risk, in a vain search after high living, of missing high thinking.[4]

Plain Living and High Thinking

"AN ideal society is that in which every individual will be able to live a life of progressively increasing wants with a minimum output of labour." Thus writes a friend. The proposition is pleasing and is backed by plausible argument which many may accept.

That everyone in this world should be able to maintain as high a standard of life as possible, with the least possible output of labour, is just as fantastic as to expect a camel to pass through the eye of a needle. The writer's high living would appear to mean luxurious living, which is an impossible proposition for any society as a whole.

And when there is no limit to luxury, where shall we stop ? All the scriptures of the world have taught the exact opposite. 'Plain living and high thinking' is the ideal that has been placed before us. The vast majority recognize its truth, but are unable to get there because of human frailty. It is, however, perfectly possible to envisage such an existence.

Man falls from the pursuit of the ideal of plain living and high thinking, the moment he wants to multiply his daily wants. History gives ample proof of this. Man's happiness really lies in contentment. He who is discontented, however much he possesses, becomes a slave to his desires. And there is really no slavery equal to that of his desires. All the sages have declared from the housetops, that the man can be his own worst enemy as well as his best friend. To be free or to be a slave lies in his own hands. And what is true for the individual, is true for the society.[5]

The Mind—A Restless Bird

THE mind is a restless bird ; the more it gets the more it wants, and still remains unsatisfied. The more we indulge our passions, the more unbridled they become. Our ancestors, therefore, set a limit to our indulgences. They saw that happiness was largely a mental condition. A man is not necessarily happy because he is rich, or unhappy because he is poor. The rich are often seen to be unhappy, the poor to be happy. Millions will always remain poor. Observing all this, our ancestors dissuaded us from luxuries and pleasures.[6]

A Delusion and a Snare

A CERTAIN degree of physical harmony and comfort is necessary, but above a certain level it becomes a hindrance instead of help. Therefore, the ideal of creating an unlimited number of wants and satisfying them seems to be a delusion and a snare. The satisfaction of one's physical needs, even the intellectual needs of one's narrow self, must meet at a certain point a dead stop, before it degenerates into physical and intellectual voluptuousness. A man must arrange his physical and cultural circumstances so that they do not hinder him in his service of humanity, on which all his energies should be concentrated.[7]

Mammon Worship

HIGH thinking is inconsistent with complicated material life based on high speed imposed on us by Mammon Worship. All the graces of life are possible only when we learn the art of living nobly.

There may be sensation in living dangerously. We must draw the distinction between living in the face of danger and living dangerously. A man who dares to live alone in the forest infested by wild beasts and wilder men without a gun and with God as his only Help, lives in the face of danger. A man who lives perpetually in mid-air and dives to the earth below to the admiration of a gaping world lives dangerously. One is a purposeful, the other a purposeless life.

Whether such plain living is possible for an isolated nation, however large geographically and numerically, in the face of a world armed to the teeth and in the midst of pomp and circumstance, is a question open to the doubt of a sceptic. The answer is straight and simple. If plain life is worth living, then the attempt is worth making even though only an individual or a group makes the effort.[8]

Dignity of Poverty

POVERTY has a dignity in our country. The poor man is not ashamed of his poverty. He prefers his hut to the rich man's palace. He even takes pride in it. Though poor in material goods, he is not poor in spirit. Contentment is his treasure. He may as well say to himself: "Since we cannot all become rich and own palaces, let us at least pull down the palaces of the rich and bring them down to our level." That can bring no happiness or peace either to themselves or anyone else, and God will certainly not be the friend and helper of the poor of such description.

Poverty, in the sense of inequality or material possessions, is there in every part of the world. That is perhaps in a certain measure inevitable, for all men are not equal either in their talents or the measure of their needs. Even in America, which is fabulously rich and where Mammon has taken the place of God, there are many poor. Poet Malabari had come across some relatives of Shah Alam begging in the streets of Rangoon. He has written a beautiful poem about it which has sunk into my heart. The substance of it is that he alone is rich who has God for his friend and helper. In India, there is a particular type of man who delights in having as few needs as possible. He carries with him only a little flour and a pinch of salt and chillies tied in his napkin. He has a **lota** and a string to draw water from the well. He needs nothing else. He walks on foot covering 10-12 miles a day. He makes the dough in his napkin, collects a few twigs to make a fire and bakes his dough on the embers. It is called **bati.** I have tasted it and found it most delicious. The relish does not lie in the food, but in the appetite that honest toil and the contentment of the mind give. Such a man has God as his companion and friend, and feels richer than any king or emperor. God is not the friend of those who inwardly covet others' riches. Everyone can copy that example and enjoy ineffable peace and happiness himself and radiate it to others. On the other hand, if one hankers after riches, one has to resort to exploitation, by whatever name it may be called. Even then, the crores cannot become millionaires. True happiness lies in contentment and companionship with God only.[9]

CHAPTER III

ON RICHES AND POVERTY

Duty of the Rich

I CANNOT picture to myself a time when no man shall be richer than another. But I do picture to myself a time when the rich will spurn to enrich themselves at the expense of the poor, and the poor will cease to envy the rich. Even in a most perfect world, we shall fail to avoid inequalities, but we can and must avoid strife and bitterness. There are numerous examples extant of the rich and the poor living in perfect friendliness. We have but to multiply such instances.[1]

I do not believe in dead uniformity.* 'All men are born equal and free' is not Nature's law in the literal sense. All men are not born equal in intellect, for instance ; but the doctrine of equality will be vindicated if those who have superior intellect will use it not for self-advancement at the expense of others, but for the service of those who are less favoured in that respect than they.[2]

While we are born equal, meaning that we have a right to equal opportunity, all have not the same capacity. It is, in the nature of things, impossible. For instance, all cannot have the same height or colour or degree of intelligence, etc. ; therefore, in the nature of things, some will have ability to earn more and others less. People with talents will have more, and they will utilize their talents for this pur-

---

* "Nor do I believe in inequalities between human beings. We are all absolutely equal. But equality is of souls and not bodies. Hence it is a mental state. We need to think of and to assert equality because we see great inequalities in the physical world. We have to realize equality in the midst of this apparent external inequality. Assumption of superiority by any person over any other is a sin against God and man."

—*Young India* : June 4, 1931.

pose. If they utilize their talents kindly, they will be performing the work of the State. Such people exist as trustees, on no other terms. I would allow a man of intellect to earn more, I would not cramp his talent. But the bulk of his greater earnings must be used for the good of the State, just as the income of all earning sons of the father goes to the common family fund. They would have their earnings only as trustees. It may be that I would fail miserably in this. But that is what I am sailing for.[3]

My Picture of Economic Equality

ECONOMIC equality of my conception does not mean that everyone would literally have the same amount. It simply means that everybody should have enough for his or her needs. For instance, I require two **shawls** in winter, whereas my grandnephew, Kanu Gandhi, who stays with me and is like my own son, does not require any warm clothing whatsoever. I require goat's milk, oranges and other fruit. Kanu can do with ordinary food. I envy Kanu, but there is no point in it. Kanu is a young man, whereas I am an old man of 76. The monthly expense of my food is far more than that of Kanu, but that does not mean that there is economic inequality between us. The elephant needs a thousand times more food than the ant, but that is not an indication of inequality. So, the real meaning of economic equality is : 'To each according to his need'. That is the definition of Marx. If a single man demands as much as a man with wife and four children, that would be a violation of economic equality.

Let no one try to justify the glaring differences between the classes and the masses, the prince and the pauper, by saying that the former need more. That will be idle sophistry and a travesty of my argument. The contrast between the rich and the poor today is a painful sight.*

---

* "The gulf that separates the rich and the poor today is appalling. It has to be bridged. The rich must share all their amenities with the poor in the fullest measure."
—*Harijan* : August 11, 1946.

The poor villagers are exploited by the foreign government and also by their own countrymen — the city-dwellers. They produce the food and go hungry. They produce milk and their children have to go without it. It is disgraceful. Everyone must have balanced diet, a decent house to live in, facilities for the education of one's children and adequate medical relief. That constitutes my picture of economic equality. I do not want to taboo everything above and beyond the bare necessaries, but they must come after the essential needs of the poor are satisfied. First things must come first.[4]

Giving up of Superfluous Possessions

THE rich have a superfluous store of things which they do not need and which are, therefore, neglected and wasted, while millions starve and are frozen to death for want of them. If each retained possession only of what he needed, no one would be in want and all would live in contentment. As it is, the rich are discontented no less than the poor. The poor man would become a millionaire and the millionaire a multi-millionaire. The poor are often not satisfied when they get just enough to fill their stomach ; but they are clearly entitled to it and society should make it a point to see that they get it. The rich must take an initiative in the matter with a view to a universal diffusion of the spirit of contentment. If only they keep their own property within moderate limits, the poor will be easily fed, and will learn the lesson of contentment along with the rich.[5]

If we wish to develop in us the capacity to look on all as equals, we should aim at getting only what the rest of the world gets. Thus, if the whole world gets milk, we may also have it. We may pray to God and say : 'O God, if you wish me to have milk, give it first to the rest of the world.' But who can pray thus ? Only he who has so much sympathy for others and who labours for their good. Even if we cannot practise this principle, we must at least understand and appreciate it. For the present, our only prayer to God should be that since we are fallen so low, He may accept whatever little we do, and that even if we do not progress in this direction, He should give us strength to lessen our possessions. If we repent for our sins, they will not increase further. We should not keep anything with us thinking it as our own, but should strive to give up as much of our possessions as we can.[6]

In my opinion, it is wrong to possess unnecessary things that presuppose defence of things possessed against those who may covet them. They require care and attention which might well be devoted to more important matters, and loss of them always leaves a pang no matter how detached you may feel about them.[7]

Defence of One's Property

THE highest fulfilment of religion requires a giving up of all possession. Having ascertained the Law of our Being, we must set about reducing it to practice to the extent of our capacity and no further. That is the middle way. When a robber comes to take away A's property, he can deliver the property to him if he recognizes in him a blood brother. If he does not feel like one, but dreads the robber and would wish that some one was near to knock him down, he must try to knock him down and take the consequence. If he has the desire but not the ability to fight the robber, he must allow himself to be robbed and then call in the assistance of law courts to regain the lost property. In both the cases, he has as good a chance of losing his property as of regaining it. If he is a sane man like me, he would reach with me the conclusion that to be really happy he must not own anything, or own things only so long as his neighbours permit him. In the last resort we live not by our physical strength, but by sufferance. Hence, the necessity of uttermost humility and absolute reliance on God. This is living by soul-force. This is highest self-expression.

Let us bear the Law in mind not as an academic and attractive proposition when it is written on paper, but as the Law of our Being to be continually realized ; and let us fashion our practice in accordance with the Law and the measure of our ability to live up to it.[8]

Advice to the Rich

THE rich should ponder well as to what is their duty today. They, who employ mercenaries to guard their wealth, may find those very guardians turning on them. The monied classes have got to learn how to fight either with arms or with the weapon of non-violence. For those who wish to follow the latter way, the best and most effective **mantra** is : तेन त्यक्तेन भुंजीथा: (Enjoy thy wealth by renouncing it). Expanded, it means : "Earn your crores by all means. But understand that your wealth is not yours ; it belongs to the people. Take what you require for your legitimate needs, and use the remainder for society." This truth has hitherto not been acted upon ; but, if the monied classes do not even act on it in these times of stress, they will remain the slaves of their riches and passions and consequently of those who overpower them.[9]

Not Necessarily Impure

Q. You say to the rich :

'Earn your crores by all means. But understand that your wealth is not yours ; it belongs to the people. Take what you require for your legitimate needs, and use the remainder for society.'

When I read this, the first question that arose in my mind was : 'Why first earn crores and then use them for society ? As society today is constituted, the means of earning crores are bound to be impure ; and one who earns crores by impure means cannot be expected to follow the **mantra** तेन त्यक्तेन भुंजीथा: because, in the very process of earning crores by impure means, the man's character is bound to be tainted or vitiated. And, moreover, you have always been emphasizing the purity of means. But I am afraid that there is a possibility of people misunderstanding that you are laying an emphasis here more on the ends than on the means.

I request you to emphasize as much, if not more, the purity of means of earning money as of spending. If purity of means is strictly observed, then, according to me, crores could not be accumulated at all and the difficulty of spending for society will assume a very minor prospect.

A. I must demur. Surely, a man may conceivably make crores through strictly pure means, assuming that a man may legitimately possess riches. For the purpose of my argument, I have assumed that private possession itself is not held to be impure. If I own a mining lease and I tumble upon a diamond of rare value, I may suddenly find myself a millionaire without being held guilty of having used impure means. This actually happened when Cullinan diamond, much more valuable than the Kohinoor, was found. Such instances can be easily multiplied. My argument was surely addressed to such men. I have no hesitation in endorsing the proposition that generally rich men, and, for that matter, most men, are not particular as to the way they make money. In the application of the method of non-violence, one must believe in the possibility of every person, however depraved, being reformed under humane and skilled treatment. We must appeal to the good in human beings and expect response. Is it not conducive to the well-being of society that every member uses all his talents, not only for personal aggrandisement but for the good of all? We do not want to produce a dead equality, where every person becomes or is rendered incapable of using his ability to the utmost possible extent. Such a society must ultimately perish. I, therefore, suggest that my advice, that monied men may earn their crores (honestly only, of course) but so as to dedicate them to the service of all, is perfectly sound. तेन त्यक्तेन भुंजीथाः is a **mantra** based on uncommon knowledge. It is the surest method to evolve a new order of life of universal benefit in the place of the present one, where each one lives for himself without regard to what happens to his neighbour.[10]

Riches v. *Poverty*

Q. How is it possible to earn lakhs in a righteous way ? Moreover, however careful a rich man is, he is bound to spend more on himself than his actual requirements merit. Therefore, why not lay more stress on **not** becoming wealthy than on trusteeship of riches ?

A. The question is apt and has been put to me before. What you could have meant was, in the **Gita** sense, that every action is tainted. It is my conviction that it is possible to acquire riches without consciously doing wrong. For example, I may light on a gold mine in my one acre of land. But I accept the proposition that it is better not to desire wealth than to acquire it and become its trustee. I gave up my own long ago, which should be proof enough of what I would like others to do. But what am I to advise those who are already wealthy, or who would not shed the desire for wealth ? I can only say to them that they should use their wealth for service. It is true that generally the rich spend more on themselves than they need. But this can be avoided. I have come across innumerable rich persons who are stingy on themselves. For some, it is part of their nature to spend next to nothing on themselves, and they do not think that they acquire merit in so doing.

The same applies to the sons of the wealthy. Personally, I do not believe in inherited riches. The well-to-do should educate and bring up their children so that they may learn how to be independent. The tragedy is that they do not do so. Their children do get some education, they even recite verses in praise of poverty, but they have no

hardly any room to sit or breathe in. Some of your pictures are hideous, not worth looking at. I recall the many restrictions that even the rich men imposed on themselves in the time of the **Mahabharata.** Let us not wear our wealth so loudly as we seem to be doing. This temperate climate of our country really does not admit of lavish display of furniture. It obstructs the free play of fresh air and it harbours dirt and so many millions of germs that float in the air. If you gave me a contract for furnishing all the rich palaces, I should give you the same things for one-tenth of the money, and give you more comfort and fresh air and secure a certificate from the best artists in India that I had furnished your houses in the most artistic manner possible. I feel that all your palaces are built anyhow without any sense of co-operation amongst yourselves and any sense of social welfare.

And you, who are rich, to you I would like to say : Whatever you do, don't spoil your purity of life. But I know that, generally speaking, it is the experience of the world that possession of gold is inconsistent with the possession of virtue ; but though such is the unfortunate experience in the world, it is by no means an inexorable law. We have the celebrated instance of Janaka, who, although he was rolling in riches and had a limitless power, being a great prince, was still one of the purest men of his age. And, even in our own age, I can cite from my own personal experience and tell you that I have the good fortune of knowing several monied men who do not find it impossible to lead a straight, pure life. What is possible for these few men is surely possible for every one of you. And I wish that my word can find an abiding place in your heart, and I know how much good it will do you and the society in which you are living.[12]

Rich Men as Trustees

Q. You have asked rich men to be trustees. It is implied that they should give up private ownership in their property and create out of it a trust valid in the eyes of the law and managed democratically? How will the successor of the present incumbent be determined on his demise?

A. I adhere to the position taken by me years before, that everything belongs to God and is from God. Therefore, it is for His people as a whole, not for a particular individual. When an individual has more than his proportionate portion, he becomes a trustee of that portion for God's people.

God, who is All-Powerful, has no need to store. He creates from day to day; hence men also shall, in theory, live from day to day and not stock things. If this truth is imbibed by the people generally, it will become legalized and trusteeship will become a legalized institution. I wish it becomes a gift from India to the world. Then there will be no exploitation and no reserves, as in Australia and other countries, for White men and their posterity. In these distinctions lies the seed of a war more virulent than the last two. As to the successor, the trustee in office will have the right to nominate his successor subject to legal sanction.[13]

Donation of Tainted Money

Q. Supposing a man has earned millions by exploiting millions of his poor brethren and made a gift of them to a **Mahatma** like you, and supposing you use that money for the benefit of humanity, is the exploiter absolved from sin? Does not some blame attach to you, too, for having accepted this ill-gotten wealth? How can one remain blameless in this unending vicious circle? How is **Ahimsa** to cope with this immoral exploitation?

A. Let us assume, for the purpose of this riddle, that I am really a **Mahatma,** and then try to solve it. The gift of what you assume to be ill-gotten gains cannot lessen the guilt of the exploiter. If he had kept the money for himself, that would have been an additional count against him. If instead he makes a gift of it to me from pure motives, he escapes the additional sin. It is also likely that a good use of his gift may wean the exploiter from immoral means of making money. But no blame attaches to me for having accepted the gift. As the foul waters from drains flowing into the sea partake of its purity, even so does tainted wealth become pure when put to the purest use. There is one condition, however, that we have assumed, **viz.,** that the gift is made and accepted out of pure motives.

Exploitation of the poor can be extinguished not by effecting the destruction of a few millionaires, but by removing the ignorance of the poor and teaching them to non-co-operate with their exploiters. That will convert the exploiters also. I have even suggested that ultimately it will lead to both being equal partners. Capital as such is not evil ; it is its wrong use that is evil. Capital, in some form or other, will always be needed.[14]

To Rich Men in Financial Trouble

Remember that :

1. He who ma... money has the right to lose it.

2. There is no shame in losing it, but to lose it and to conceal the losses is both shameful and sinful.

3. Never live beyond your means. Live in a palace today, but be in readiness to live in a hut tomorrow.

4. There is nothing to be ashamed of, if you have not enough money to pay creditors off.

5. A debtor, who hands over all his possessions to his creditors, has paid them in full.

6. Never carry on trade with borrowed money — this is the first principle. The second is to give the lenders all you have and have done with it.[15]

CHAPTER IV

ON NECESSITY OF 'BREAD-LABOUR'

'By the Sweat of Thy Brow'

'EARN thy bread by the sweat of thy brow,' says the Bible. If all laboured for their bread and no more, then there would be enough food and enough leisure for all. Then, there would be no cry of over-population, no disease, and no such misery as we see around. Such labour will be the highest form of sacrifice. Men will, no doubt, do many other things either through their bodies or through their minds, but all this will be labour of love for the common good. There will be then no rich and no poor, none high and none low, no touchable and no untouchable.

This may be an unattainable ideal. But we need not, therefore, cease to strive for it. Even if without fulfilling the whole Law of Sacrifice, that is, the Law of our Being, we performed physical labour enough for our daily bread, we should go a long way towards the Ideal.

If we did so, our wants would be minimized, our food would be simple. We should then eat to live, not live to eat. Let anyone who doubts the accuracy of this proposition try to sweat for his bread, he will derive the greatest relish from the production of his labour, improve his health and discover that many things he took were superfluities.

May not men earn their bread by intellectual labour? No. The needs of the body must be supplied by the body. 'Render unto Caesar that which is Caesar's', perhaps applies here as well.

Mere mental, that is, intellectual labour is for the soul and is its own satisfaction. It should never demand payment. In the ideal state, doctors, lawyers and the like will work solely for the benefit of society, not for self. Obedience to the Law of Bread-Labour will bring about a silent revolution in the structure of society. Man's triumph will consist in substituting the struggle for existence by the struggle for mutual service. The Law of the Brute will be replaced by the Law of Man.

Compulsory obedience to a master is a state of slavery ; willing obedience to one's father is the glory of sonship. Similarly, compulsory obedience to the Law of Bread-Labour breeds poverty, disease and discontent, it is a state of slavery. Willing obedience to it must bring contentment and health. And it is health which is real wealth, not pieces of silver and gold.[1]

If everybody lived by the sweat of his brow, the earth would become a paradise. The question of the use of special talents hardly needs separate consideration. If everyone labours physically for his bread, it follows that poets, doctors, lawyers etc., will regard it their duty to use those talents **gratis** for the service of humanity. Their output will be all the better and richer for their selfless devotion to duty.[2]

Educative Value of Manual Work

I AM a firm believer in the educative value of manual work. Useful manual labour, intelligently performed, is the means **par excellence** for developing the intellect. One may develop a sharp intellect otherwise, too. But, then, it will not be a balanced growth but an unbalanced, distorted abortion. It might easily make of one a rogue and a rascal. A balanced intellect presupposes a harmonious growth of body, mind and soul. An intellect that is developed through the medium of socially useful labour will be an instrument for service, and will not easily be led astray or fall into devious paths. The latter can well be a scourge.[3]

Intellectual and Manual Work

INTELLECTUAL work is important and has an undoubted place in the scheme of life. But what I insist on is the necessity of physical labour. No man, I claim, ought to be free from that obligation. It will serve to improve even the quality of his intellectual output. I venture to say that in ancient times **Brahmins** worked with their body as with their mind. But even if they did not, body-labour is a proved necessity at the present time. In this connection, I would refer to the life of Tolstoy and how he made famous the theory of Bread-Labour, first propounded in his country by the Russian peasant, Bondaref.[4]

Poetry of the Five Fingers

OUR education has got to be revolutionized. The brain must be educated through the hand. If I were a poet, I would write poetry of the possibilities of the five fingers. Why should you think that the mind is everything and the hands and feet nothing? Those who do not train their hands, who go through the ordinary run of education, lack 'music' in their life. All their faculties are not trained. Mere book knowledge does not interest the child so as to hold his attention fully. The brain gets weary of mere words, and the child's mind begins to wander. The hand does the things it ought not to do; the eye sees the things it ought not to see; the ear hears the things it ought not to hear; and they do not do, see, or hear, respectively, what they ought to. They are not taught to make the right choice, and so their education often proves their ruin. An education which does not teach us to discriminate between good and bad, to assimilate the one and eschew the other, is a misnomer.[5]

CHAPTER V

ON THE ART OF STANDING ALONE

Art of Standing Alone

IN every great cause, it is not the number of figures that counts, but it is the quality of which they are made that becomes the deciding factor. The greatest men of the world have always stood alone. Take the great prophets, Zoroaster, Buddha, Jesus, Mohammed — they all stood alone like many others whom I can name. But they had living faith in themselves and their God, and, believing as they did that God was on their side, they never felt lonely. You may recall the occasion when pursued by numerous enemies, Abu Bakr, who was accompanying the Prophet in his flight, trembled to think of their fate and said : 'Look at the number of the enemies that is overtaking us. What shall we two do against these heavy odds?' Without a moment's reflection, the Prophet rebuked his faithful companion by saying : 'No, Abu Bakr, we are three, for God is with us.' Or, take the invisible faith of Vibhishan and Prahlad. I want you to have that same living faith in yourself and God.[1]

Strength of Numbers

PRAYERFUL, well-meaning effort never goes in vain, and man's success lies only in such an effort. The result is in His hands.

Strength of numbers is the delight of the timid. The valiant of spirit glory in fighting alone. Be you one or many, this valour is the only true valour, all else is false. And the valour of the spirit cannot be achieved without sacrifice, determination, faith and humility.[2]

The history of great deeds was the history of men who

had the courage to stand alone against the world. Krishna was alone sufficient to inspire the wavering hosts by his presence ; he never relied on the strength of numbers. The Prophet touched the high water-mark of his greatness, not when he was acclaimed by Arabia as the all-conquering hero, but when he was glad to stand by God in a minority of one. Pratap, deserted by all, carried on alone a desperate and losing fight to his dying day but refused to lower the flag for a single second ; even so did Shivaji, and the world remembers their names with pride.[3]

Futility of Mere Numbers

WE have an ocular demonstration of the futility of mere numbers before us every day. The very sight of a lion puts to flight a thousand sheep. The reason is plain. The sheep are aware of their weakness, the lion of its strength. And the consciousness of strength in the latter overpowers the numerical strength of the former. By analogy, may we not deduce that 'soul force' or 'spirit force' may not after all be a mere chimera or figment of imagination but a substantial reality ?

I do not wish to disparage the strength of numbers. It has its use, but only when it is backed by the latent spirit-force. Millions of ants can kill an elephant by together attacking it in a vulnerable place. Their sense of solidarity, consciousness of oneness of spirit in spite of the diversity of bodies, in other words, their spirit-force makes the ants irresistible. Even so, the moment we develop a sense of mass-unity like the ants, we, too, shall become irresistible. That quality is more than quantity is a sound theory, because it is true in practice. Indeed, I hold that what cannot be proved in practice, cannot be sound in theory.

When Galileo declared that the earth was round like a ball and turned on its axis, he was ridiculed as a visionary and a dreamer and was greeted with abuse. But today we know that Galileo was right, and it was his opponents, who believed the earth to be stationary and flat like a dish, that were living in the cloudland of their ignorance.

Modern education tends to turn our eyes away from the spirit. The possibilities of the spirit-force or soul-force, therefore, do not appeal to us, and our eyes are consequently rivetted on the evanescent, transitory, material force. Surely, this is the very limit of dull unimaginativeness.[4]

I Plead for Quality

I ATTACH the highest importance to quality irrespective almost of quantity, the more so for Indian conditions. In the midst of suspicion, discord, antagonistic interests, superstition, fear, distrust and the like, there is not only no safety in numbers but there may be even danger in them. Who does not know how often numbers have embarrassed us? Numbers become irresistible when they act as one man under exact discipline. They are a self-destroying force when each pulls his own way, or when no one knows which way to pull.

I am convinced that there is safety in fewness so long as we have not evolved cohesion, exactness and intelligent co-operation and responsiveness. One virtuous son is better than one hundred loafers. Five Pandavas were more than a match for one hundred Kauravas. A disciplined army of a few hundred picked men has, times without number, routed countless undisciplined hordes. I plead for quality and quality alone.[5]

I believe in quality rather than quantity. The fashion nowadays is to rely upon quantity even at the cost of quality. Quantity has its place no doubt in social and political economy. Only, I am ill-fitted for organizing quantity in the way it is done at present.[6]

Not Quantity But Quality

TIMES without number have I been asked : 'What can be done if we are so few. See, how few spinners we have in the Spinners' Association ? How few civil resisters ? How few **pucca** non-co-operators ? How few prohibitionists ?' All this is, alas, too true. But when we come to think of it, what is there in numbers ? The more relevant question is : How many true spinners, true civil resisters, true non-co-operators, true prohibitionists are there in the country ? It is character, determination, and courage that will count in the end.

One is told that the revolution in Japan was brought about not through thousands of men, but at the head of it were only 12 men who fired the zeal of fifty-five. And probably amongst these 12, was only one man who was the author of the whole plan. If a true beginning is made, the rest is simple. We, therefore, arrive at the astonishing conclusion, which is nonetheless true, that one true man is enough for any reform no matter how impossible it may appear in the beginning. Ridicule, contempt and death may be and often is the reward of such a man. But though he may die, the reforms survive and prosper. He ensures their stability with his blood. I wish, therefore, that workers will think less of numbers irrespective of strength, but more of the strength of the few. It is depth more than the width that is wanted. If we lay a stable foundation, posterity will be able to erect a solid structure upon ; whereas, if the foundation is built on sand, there will be no work for posterity except to dig out the sand to lay the foundation anew.[7]

CHAPTER VI

ON SELF-HELP AND MUTUAL HELP

SELF-HELP is the capacity to stand on one's legs without anybody's help. This does not mean indifference to or rejection of outside help ; but it means the capacity to be at peace with oneself, to preserve one's self-respect, when outside help is not forthcoming or is refused. A farmer who, rejecting friends' help, insists on tilling his own soil, making his own implements, gathering his own harvest, spinning and weaving his own cloth and building his own house, all by himself, must be either foolish or self-conceited or barbarous. Self-help includes bread-labour and means that every man shall earn his bread in the sweat of his brow. Hence, a man who works in his field for eight hours daily is entitled to help from the weaver, the carpenter, the blacksmith or the mason. It is not only his right, it is his duty to seek the help of these, and they, in their turn, benefit by the agriculturist's labour in the field. The eye that would dispense with the help of the hands does not practise self-help, but is conceited and self-deprived. And as the different members of the body are self-reliant, so far as their own functions are concerned, and yet are mutually helpful and mutually dependent, so are we three hundred million members of the Indian body politic, each following the rule of self-help in performing his own function, and yet co-operating with one another in all matters of common interest. Only then can we be said to be servants of the country and only then do we deserve to be called nationalists.[1]

Interdependence

MAN is a social being. Without interrelation with society, he cannot realize his oneness with the universe or suppress his egotism. His social interdependence enables him to test his faith and to prove himself on the touchstone of reality. If man were so placed or could so place himself as to be absolutely above all dependence on his fellow-beings, he would become so proud and arrogant as to be a veritable burden and nuisance to the world. Dependence on society teaches him the lesson of humility. That a man ought to be able to satisfy most of his essential needs himself is obvious ; but it is no less obvious to me that when self-sufficiency is carried to the length of isolating oneself from society, it almost amounts to sin. A man cannot become self-sufficient even in respect of all the various operations, from the growing of cotton to the spinning of the yarn. He has, at some stage or other, to take the aid of the members of his family. And if one may take help from one's own family, why not from one's neighbours ? Or otherwise, what is the significance of the great saying : 'The world is my family' ?

Fanatical excess is a thing always to be shunned. The 'middle path' is the royal road. Self-dependence is a necessary ideal so long as, and to the extent that it is an aid to one's self-respect and spiritual discipline It becomes an obsession and a hindrance, when it is pushed beyond that limit. On the other hand, interdependence, when it is not inconsistent with one's self-respect, is necessary to bring home to man the lesson of humility and the omnipotence of God. One must strike a golden mean between these two extremes. A fanaticism that refuses to discriminate is the negation of all ideal.[2]

Let us not also forget that it is man's social nature which distinguishes him from the brute creation. If it is his privilege to be independent, it is equally his duty to be interdependent. Only an arrogant man will claim to be independent of everybody else and be self-contained.[3]

True Co-operation

INDIVIDUAL liberty and interdependence are both essential for life in society. Only a Robinson Crusoe can afford to be all self-sufficient. When a man has done all he can for the satisfaction of his essential requirements, he will seek the co-operation of his neighbours for the rest. That will be true co-operation.[4]

There are limits to the capacity of an individual, and the moment he flatters himself that he can undertake all tasks, God is there to humble his pride. For myself, I am gifted with enough humility to look even to babes and sucklings for help.[5]

CHAPTER VII

ON WORKING WITH DETACHMENT

Renunciation v. Action

I BELIEVE in the doctrine of renunciation, but I hold that renunciation should be sought for in and through action. That action is the **sine qua non** of life in the body, that the Wheel of Life cannot go on even for a second without involving some sort of action goes without saying. Renunciation can, therefore, in these circumstances, only mean detachment or freedom of the spirit from action, even while the body is engaged in action. A follower of the path of renunciation seeks to attain it not by refraining from all activity, but by carrying it on in a perfect spirit of detachment and altruism as a pure trust. Thus, a man may engage in farming, spinning, or any other activity without departing from the path of renunciation, provided one does so merely for selfless service and remains from the taint of egoism or attachment. It remains for those, therefore, who like myself hold this view of renunciation to discover for themselves how far the principle of **Ahimsa** is compatible with life in the body, and how it can be applied to acts of everyday life. The very virtue of a **dharma** is that it is universal, that its practice is not the monopoly of the few, but must be the privilege of all. And it is my firm belief that the scope of Truth and **Ahimsa** is world-wide. That is why I find an ineffable joy in dedicating my life to researches in Truth and **Ahimsa** and I invite others to share it with me by doing likewise.[1]

Work With Detachment

IF you work with detachment, you will refuse to be rushed and you will refuse to let anything get on your nerves. Having put one's whole heart into a thing entrusted or undertaken, one can leave the result to God. Then, there can be no rush and no worry. You know the story of King Janaka. He was Duty personified. His capital was in flames. He knew it. But some busybody reported it to him. His answer was : 'What care I whether my capital is reduced to ashes or remains intact !' He had done all he could to save it. His going to the sense of operations and fussing would have distracted the attention of the fire-brigade and others and made matters worse. He was but an agent of Providence. As such, he had done his part and was, therefore, quiet and at ease. So may, must we be, if we have done our best, whether our work flourishes or perishes.[2]

'Be careful for nothing'. 'Look at the lilies of the field. They toil not, neither do they spin ; and yet Solomon in all his glory was not arrayed like one of these'. I do not know whether I have quoted correctly. Anyhow, the lilies only **seem** neither to toil nor to spin. They do both, but so naturally that we do not notice their toilsome spin. If they did not toil, they would wither. Only they have not the egotism and hence attachments, likes and dislikes that we have. But when we toil like them detachedly, our toil will not be noticed and, therefore, will not adversely affect the body. All of us have to make a conscious and deliberate effort to realize this blessed state.[3]

A Scientific Necessity

EVERY sickness leaves behind it a legacy of weakness, unless the system is allowed full rest and the mind relieved of tension. I suppose the mental control is the most difficult. For this, the sovereign remedy is the application of the **Gita.** Each time the mind suffers a shock, there is failure in application. Let good news as well as bad pass over like water over a duck's back. When we hear any, our duty is merely to find out whether any action is necessary and, if it is, to do it as an instrument in the hands of Nature without being affected by or attached to the result. This detachment appears a scientific necessity, when we remember that in bringing about a result more than one instrument is employed. Who shall dare say : 'I have done it' ?

I drive the truth home, so that from the brain it may percolate to the heart. So long as it remains in the brain only, it is a dead weight on it. Any truth received by the brain must immediately be sent down to the heart. When it is not, it suffers abortion and then it lies on the brain as so much poisonous matter. What poisons the brain, poisons the whole system. Hence, the necessity of using the brain, as it should be, merely as a transmitting station. Whatever is there received is either transmitted to the heart for immediate action, or it is rejected there and then as being unfit for transmission. Failure of the brain to perform this function properly is the cause of almost all the ills that flesh is heir to, as also for mental exhaustion. If the brain simply performed its function, there need never by any brain-fag. So, whenever we suffer from illness, generally there is not only a dietetic error, but there is also failure on the part of the brain to function properly. The author of the **Gita** evidently saw this and gave the world the sovereign remedy in the clearest possible language. Whenever, therefore, anything preys upon your mind, you should meditate on the central teaching of the **Gita** and throw off the burden.[4]

Rest in the Spirit of Service

WHY should rest not be taken in the spirit of service ? Of course, it can be easily abused and often is. But that is no reason why honest people may not honestly give themselves rest, so as to enable them to keep fit for further service. I regard it as self-delusion, if not worse, when a person says he is wearing himself away in service. Is such service preferred by God to service steadily and detachedly performed? Body is like a machine requiring to be well kept for full service. Rest, properly and in due time taken, is like the proverbial timely stitch.[5]

The English Detachment

I HAVE often expressed the opinion among friends that, in the matter of capacity for detachment, Englishmen are far in advance of us. No matter how important national affairs may be, they will keep their meal hours and hours of recreation. They are not unnerved in the face of dangers or impending calamity. This may be called working in the spirit of the **Gita.** Among the political workers in India, there are few who come up to the Englishmen's standard.

This English detachment is worthy of emulation. That it is used for the exploitation of the so-called uncivilized or semi-civilized races of the earth, is another matter. It would be a distinct gain to the national cause, if the leaders and workers strictly keep their hours. No man is expected to do more than he really can. If, at the end of the day, there is surplus work left, or he cannot get through it without missing a meal or encroaching upon the hours of sleep or recreation, there is mismanagement somewhere. I have no doubt that if we cultivate the habit of punctuality and acting according to programme, the index of national efficiency will go up, our advance towards our goal will be rapid, and the workers will be healthier and longer lived.[6]

CHAPTER VIII

ON RIGHTS AND DUTIES

True Source of Rights

THE true source of rights is duty. If we all discharge our duties, rights will not be far to seek. If leaving duties unperformed we run after rights, they will escape us like a will o' the wisp. The more we pursue them, the farther will they fly. The same teaching has been embodied by Krishna in the immortal words : 'Action alone is thine. Leave thou the fruit severely alone.' Action is duty ; fruit is the right.[1]

No people have risen who thought only of rights. Only those did so, who thought of duties. Out of the performance of duties flow rights, and those that knew and performed their duties came naturally by the rights. The **Shastras** inculcate reverence to parents. It means implicit obedience to them, and why do we willingly obey like that ? We know that an angry look from his mother was sufficient to make the giant-like Shaukat Ali cower before her. What is the secret of his willing obedience ? It is that the obedience carries with it enjoyment of a right—the right to inheritance. At the back of obedience is a consciousness of a right to be enjoyed, and yet woe to the man who obeys with an eye to the right to inheritance. It is the **Shastras** again that inculcate obedience without an eye to the fruit thereof. He who thinks not of the right, gets it; and he who thinks of it, loses it. That is the rule of conduct I would like to place before you.[2]

Performance of One's Duty

PERFORMANCE of one't's duty should be independent of public opinion. I have all along held that one is bound to act according to what to one appears to be right, even though it may appear wrong to others. And experience has shewn that that is the only correct course. I admit that there is always a possibility of one's mistaking right for wrong and **vice versa,** but often one learns to recognize wrong only through unconscious error. On the other hand, if a man fails to follow the Light within for fear of public opinion or any other similar reason, he would never be able to know right from wrong and in the end lose all sense of distinction between the two. That is why the poet has sung :

> "The pathway of Love is the ordeal of fire,
> The shrinkers turn away from it."

The pathway of **Ahimsa,** that is, of Love, one has often to tread all along.[3]

We Rise Through Suffering

WE rise through our suffering. That is Nature's law. He who clings to his sordid self or family interests loses. Man is sent into the world to perform his duty even at the cost of his life, if necessary. We must, therefore, be braced for any suffering that may come in the performance of duty.[4]

He who invites suffering may not complain about it even to himself. On the other hand, suffering should be to him as happiness. In what an ecstasy did Sudhanva dance in the pan of hot oil ! Let us not dismiss them as the heroes of idle myths, for their experience can be ours today. Latimer and Ridley and Mansur are all historic persons. It all depends upon the mind.

To draw suffering on oneself when misfortune dogs one's footsteps is no novelty. How did Prahlad embrace a pillar of red-hot iron ?[3]

Give Up Rights But Not Duties

A MAN can give up a right, but he may not give up a duty without being guilty of a grave dereliction. Unpopularity and censure are often the lot of a man who wants to speak and practise the Truth. I hold it to be the bounden duty of a **Satyagrahi** openly and freely to express his opinions which he holds to be correct and of benefit to the public even at the risk of incurring popular displeasure and worse. So long as I believe my views on **Ahimsa** to be correct, it would be a sin of omission on my part not to give expression to them.[6]

One, therefore, need not be deterred from doing what one considers to be right, merely because one's conduct may be misunderstood or misinterpreted by others.[7]

Duty Creates A Corresponding Right

EVERY duty performed confers upon one certain rights, whilst the exercise of every right carries with it certain corresponding obligations. And so the never ending cycle of duty and right goes ceaselessly on.[8]

There is no duty but creates a corresponding right, and those only are true rights which flow from a due performance of one's duties. Hence, rights of true citizenship accrue only to those who serve the State to which they belong. And they alone can do justice to the rights that accrue to them. Everyone possesses the right to tell lies or resort to **goondaism.** But the exercise of such a right is harmful both to the exerciser and society. But to him, who observes Truth and Non-violence, comes prestige; and prestige brings rights. And people who obtain rights as a result of performance of duty, exercise them only for the service of society, never for themselves.[9]

Proved right should be capable of being vindicated by right means as against the rude, **i.e.,** sanguinary, means. Man may, and should, shed his own blood for establishing what he considers to be his 'right'. He may not shed the blood of his opponent who disputes his 'right'.[10]

Rights accrue automatically to him who duly performs his duties. In fact, the right to perform one's duties is the only right that is worth living for and dying for. It covers all legitimate rights. All the rest is garb under one guise or another and contains in it seeds of **himsa**.[11]

All rights to be deserved and preserved come from duty well done. Thus, the very right to live accrues to us only when we do the duty of citizenship of the world. From this very fundamental statement, perhaps, it is easy enough to define the duties of man and woman and correlate every right to some corresponding duty to be first performed. Every other right can be shown to be an usurpation, hardly worth fighting for.[12]

Duty well done undoubtedly carries rights with it; but a man who discharges his obligations with an eye upon privileges, generally discharges them indifferently and often fails to attain the rights he might have expected; or when he succeeds in gaining them, they turn out to be burdens.[13]

Rights or Duties ?

IF, instead of insisting on rights, everyone does his duty, there will immediately be the rule of order established among mankind. There is no such thing as the divine right of kings to rule and the humble duty of the **ryots** to pay respectful obedience to their masters. Whilst it is true that these hereditary inequalities must go, as being injurious to the well-being of society, the unabashed assertion of rights of the hitherto down-trodden millions is equally injurious, if not more so, to the same well-being. The latter behaviour is probably calculated to injure the millions rather than the few claimants of divine or other rights. They could but die a brave or cowardly death, but those few dead would not bring in the orderly life of blissful contentment. It is, therefore, necessary to understand the correlation of rights and duties.

I venture to suggest that rights, that do not flow directly from duty well performed, are not worth having. They will be usurpations, sooner discarded the better. A wretched parent, who claims obedience from his children without first doing his duty by them, excites nothing but contempt. It is distortion of religious precept for a dissolute husband to expect compliance in every respect from his dutiful wife. But the children who flout their parent, who is ever ready to do his duty towards them, would be considered ungrateful and would harm themselves more than their parent. The same can be said about husband and wife.

If you apply this simple and universal rule to employers and labourers, landlords and tenants, the princes and their subjects, you will find that the happiest relations can be established in all walks of life without creating disturbance in, and dislocation of, life and business which you see in India as in the other parts of the world.[14]

Violence Defends No Right

Q. Cannot a person whose right is in danger defend it violently ?

A. Violence, in reality, defends no right and no one. If every right flows from duty well performed, then it is unassailable. Thus, I have a right to my wage only when I have fully performed the duty undertaken by me. If I take the wage without doing my work, it becomes theft. I cannot associate myself with continuous insistence on rights without reference to the performance of duties, on which the rights depend and from which they flow.[15]

I hold, too, that every right carries with it a duty; better still, there is no right which does not flow from duty duly performed.[16]

CHAPTER IX

ON MEANS AND ENDS

Impure Means Result in Impure End

IMPURE means result in an impure end. One cannot reach Truth by untruthfulness. Truthful conduct alone can reach Truth. Are not Non-violence and Truth twins ? The answer is an emphatic 'No'. Non-violence is embedded in Truth and **vice versa.** Hence has it been said that they are faces of the same coin. Either is inseparable from the other. Read the coin either way. The spelling of words will be different. The value is the same. This blessed state is unattainable without perfect purity. Harbour impurity of mind or body and you have untruth and violence in you.[1]

The means may be likened to a seed, the end to a tree; and there is just the same inviolable connection between the means and the end, as there is between the seed and the tree.[2]

As the Means, So the End

THEY say : 'means are after all means.' I would say : 'means are after all everything.' As the means, so the end. There is no wall of separation between means and end. Indeed, the Creator has given us control (and that, too, very limited) over means, none over the end. Realization of the goal is in exact proportion to that of the means. This is a proposition that admits of no exception.[3]

' To work thou hast the right, never to the fruit thereof ' is one of the golden precepts of the **Gita.**[4]

We are merely the instruments of the Almighty's will and are, therefore, ignorant of what helps us forward and what acts as an impediment. We must thus rest satisfied with a knowledge only of the means, and if these are pure, we can fearlessly leave the end to take care of itself.[5]

For me, it is enough to know the means. Means and end are convertible terms in my philosophy of life.[6]

Be Concerned About the Means

FOR over 50 years, I have trained myself never to be concerned about the result. What I should be concerned about is the means ; and when I am sure of the purity of the means, faith is enough to lead me on. All fear and trembling melt away before that faith ; and once we have launched forth, there is no looking back.[7]

We should do our duty and leave the results in the hands of God,* and not in the hands of man. Man is supposed to be the maker of his own destiny. It is partly true. He can make his destiny only in so far as he is allowed by the Great Power which overrides all our intentions, all our plans and carries out His own plans.

I call that Great Power not by the name of **Allah,** not by the name of **Khuda** or God, but by the name of Truth. For me, Truth is God and Truth overrides all our plans. The whole truth is only embodied within the heart of that Great Power—Truth. I was taught from my early days to regai Truth as unapproachable—something that you cannot reach. A great Englishman taught me to believe that God is unknowable. He is knowable, but knowable only to the extent that our limited intellect allows.[8]

Right Conduct

RIGHT conduct is not like Euclid's right line. It is like a beautiful tree, not one of whose millions of leaves is like any other. Though, therefore, they are from one seed and

---

* "Success or failure is not in our hands. It is enough we do our part well. Ours is but to strive. In the end, it will be as He wishes."
—*Harijan* : January 12, 1948.

belong to the same tree, there is none of the uniformity of a geometrical figure about any part of a tree. And yet we know that the seed, the branches and the leaves are one and the same. We know, too, that no geometrical figure can bear comparison with a full-blossomed tree in point of beauty and grandeur.[9]

CHAPTER X

ON HONESTY IN BUSINESS AND LIFE

Business and Ethics

IT is wrong to think that business is incompatible with ethics. I know that it is perfectly possible to carry one's business profitably and yet honestly and truthfully. The plea that business and ethics never agree is advanced only by those who are actuated by nothing higher than narrow self-interest. He who will serve his own ends will do so by all kinds of questionable means, but he who will earn to serve the community will never sacrifice truth or honesty. You must bear in mind that you have the right to earn as much as you like, but not the right to spend as much as you like. Anything that remains after the needs of a decent living are satisfied, belongs to the community.[1]

Dishonest Practices in Business

I DO not hold dishonest practices in business to be warranted or excusable. The principle of unconditional honesty is as binding in this as in any other field of life, and it is up to a businessman never to compromise his principle, no matter what it may cost him. In the end, of course, honesty pays, though that can hardly be a consideration for observing it. One has a perfect right to fix and regulate the scale of prices that he shall charge from a particular set of customers, but it must be done according to a clear fixed principle and not out of mere opportunism or immoral expediency. There should be in it no room for fraud, sharp practice or finesse to bamboozle the simple, unsuspecting customer.[2]

Does Dishonesty Win in Life?

Q. Is it not a fact that untruth and dishonesty often win in life?

A. That certainly is not my experience. They often **seem** to win, but if you dive a little deeper you will find that, in reality, Truth wins. But if the victory of Truth was always easy and self-evident, Truth would not have the value it has, and the observance of Truth would be no merit. The way of Truth is straight and narrow, and it is our duty to point it out whenever there is an opportunity. We do not always know wherein lies our good. That is why it is best to assume that good always comes from following the path of Truth.[3]

The Way of Truth and Non-violence

THE way of Non-violence and Truth is sharp as the razor's edge. Its practice is more than our daily food. Rightly taken, food sustains the body ; rightly practised, Non-violence sustains the soul. The body food we can only take in measured quantities and at stated intervals ; Non-violence, which is the spiritual food, we have to take in continually. There is no such thing as satiation.[4]

How can inconcrete entities like Truth and Non-violence be organized ? I maintain that they can be so organized. Otherwise, they would, for me, cease to be eternal principles. An eternal principle, as the Jains say, has no exceptions. Truth and Non-violence are thus no cloistered virtues, but applicable as much in the forum and the legislatures as in the market place.

Truth and Non-violence are not for the dense. Pursuit of them is bound to result in an all-round growth of the body, mind and heart. If this does not follow, either Truth and Non-violence are untrue or we are untrue ; and since the former is impossible, the latter will be the only conclusion.[5]

Honesty is the Best Policy

Q. I am a young businessman of 21 years and have 11 dependants. I believe in Truth and Non-violence, but find I cannot strictly follow it in business. What should I do ? Abandoning the business means suffering for my relations.

A. This begs the question. It is difficult but not impossible to conduct strictly honest business. The fact is that the honester a business, the more successful it is. Hence, the proverb coined by the businessman : "Honesty is the best policy ". What the correspondent lacks is application and an accurate knowledge of honest business methods. What is true is that honesty is incompatible with the amassing of a large fortune. "Verily, verily, it is easier for a camel to go through the eye of a needle than for a rich man to enter into the Kingdom of God." Nor, therefore, should an honest businessman, however capable he may be, support idlers whether eleven or more or fewer. The eleven dependants cannot all be infants or incapables. Honesty makes no impossible demands upon the resources of a businessman. An honest man cannot have dishonest kinsmen. The questioner will find on introspection that there is nothing wrong with honest business, but that there is something wrong with him. Let him find out what it is that is wrong with him.

Q. Trade is impossible without telling lies. What am I to do ? I cannot think of any other occupation suitable for myself.

A. The man of Truth is he who will tell and practise the Truth, no matter in what circumstances he is placed. No one is bound to tell lies whether in trade or in service. But if we are compelled to tell a lie anywhere, we must not accept such work and not mind even if we starve without it.[7]

Orthodox Conception of Redemption

THE orthodox conception of redemption is redemption in the life to come. What I want to tell you is that redemption is promised us here and now, if we fulfil the necessary conditions. They are, firstly, self-purification and, secondly, obedience to the Law. It is vain, it is demoralizing to expect that in the life to come God will vindicate His title as Redeemer by saving us, while we continue to carry the load of sin on our heads in this life. A businessman who lies and cheats his simple-minded, ignorant customers cannot hope to be saved.[8]

A Question

Q. Can a man, who resorts to untruth for worldly purposes, see God ? Or, is the Beatific Vision possible for one who gives up all activities in order to be able to observe the Law of Truth ?

A. One who resorts to untruth, with any end in view whatsoever, and is full of likes and dislikes can never attain the Supreme. Your second question deals with an impossibility. To tread the path of Truth and to eschew all activity— this is a contradiction in terms. If a man is not active, how can we say anything about the path he has taken ? To tread the path of Truth implies an active life in the world of men. In the absence of such activity, there is no occasion for either pursuing or swerving from Truth. The **Gita** has made it clear that a man cannot remain inactive even for a single moment. The difference between one who is a devotee of God and another who is not, is that the former is active in the service of others, never gives up Truth in the midst of activity and gradually overcomes his likes and dislikes; while the other is active for selfish reasons and has no scruples whatever as regards the means he employs in order to achieve his selfish ends. This world is not something evil in itself, for only an active life in the world can help us to attain the goal of God-Realization. This activity must be directed to the good of others. Selfish activity is fit only to be condemned and should be given up.[9]

CHAPTER XI

ON SERVICE AND SELF-SACRIFICE

Meaning and Worth of Life

LIFE for me is real as I believe it to be a spark of the Divine.

Religion, not in the conventional but in the broadest sense, helps me to have a glimpse of the Divine Essence. This glimpse is impossible without full development of the moral sense. Hence, religion and morality are, for me, synonymous terms.

Striving for full realization keeps me going.

This strife is the source of whatever inspiration and energy I possess.

My consolation and my happiness are to be found in service of all that lives, because the Divine Essence is the sum-total of all life.

My pleasure lies in battling against darkness and all forces of evil.[1]

Man's Ultimate Aim

MAN'S ultimate aim is the realization of God, and all his activities, social, political, religious, have to be guided by the ultimate aim of the vision of God. The immediate service of all human beings becomes a necessary part of the endeavour, simply because the only way to find God is to see Him in His creation and be one with it. This can only be done by service of all.[2]

The purpose of life is undoubtedly to know oneself. We cannot do it unless we learn to identify ourselves with all that lives. The sum-total of that life is God. Hence, the necessity of realizing God living within every one of us.

Job :

Man that is born of a woman is of few days,
    and full of trouble,
He cometh forth like a flower, and is cut
    down; he fleeth also as a shadow,
    and continueth not ;
Seeing his days are determined, the number
    of his months are with Thee; Thou
    hast appointed his bounds that he cannot pass;
For, there is hope of a tree, if it be cut down,
    that it will sprout again and that the
    tender branch thereof will not cease;
Though the root thereof wax old in the earth,
    and the stock thereof die in the ground;
Yet through the scent of water it will land,
    and bring forth boughs like a plant;
But man dieth, and wasteth away,
    Yea, man giveth up the ghost, and where is he ?
As the waters fail from the sea, and the flood
    decayeth and drieth up;
So man lieth down, and riseth not;
    till the heavens be no more, they shall
    not awake, nor be raised out of their sleep.

Psalm :

Lord, make me to know mine end and the measure
    of my days what it is, that I may know
    how frail I am.
Behold, Thou hast made my days as an hand-breadth ;
    and my age is as nothing before Thee;
    verily, every man at his best state is
    altogether vanity;
For, He knoweth our frame; He remembereth that
    we are dust;
As for man, his days are grass: as a flower of
    the field he flourisheth;
For, the wind passeth over it and it is gone ;
    and the place thereof shall know it no more.[12]

Working for the Good of Others

MAN should earnestly desire the well-being of all God's
creation and pray that he may have the strength to do so.
In desiring the well-being of all, lies his own welfare; he,
who desires only his own or his community's welfare, is
selfish and it can never be well with him. It is essential

for man to discriminate between what he may consider to be good and what is really good for him.[13]

We should learn to practise **Dharma**. **Dharma** is benevolence ; and benevolence means desiring and working for the good of others, serving them. Begin this service by loving one another, and by sharing one another's grief. But this is one and the same thing.[14]

Sacrifice in the Cause of Service

WE may not have sufficient health, ability or knowledge of letters for doing such work. But if we have pure devotion all else will follow. Devotion means faith—faith in God and in one's self. Such faith will lead one to make all sacrifices. Sacrifice, for the sake of sacrifice, is difficult ; but if it is made in the cause of service, it is easy. No mother would sleep in the wet deliberately. But she would gladly do so, if she can thereby make her child sleep in dry place.

In our work we should develop the **Gita** attitude which we desire to possess. That attitude is that whatever we do, we do selflessly in a spirit of service. Spirit of service means in a spirit of dedication to God. One who does so, loses all idea of self. He has no hatred for anybody. On the contrary, he is generous to others. Even in regard to the smallest piece of service you render, ask yourselves from time to time whether you exhibit all these qualities.[15]

Greed for Service

GREED for service has its limits. There is no end of misery in the world, if we look for it. At every step, we find there is scope for reform. Surely, God does not expect us to redress all these wrongs. But if He has any such expectations, He has also taught us the art of doing it, and it is this : We must pick up even a little bit from that mountain of misery, apply our whole mind to the task of removing it and refuse to do anything else. Having done this, we have as good as lifted the whole of the mountain.[18]

Do Only What Is Possible

IF the world is on fire, we cannot extinguish it by our impatience. In fact, it is not for us to extinguish it at all. Do you know that when there is a big blaze, the firemen do not waste any water on it at all. They only try to save the neighbourhood; and if they succeed in saving it, they are **yogis**—skilful in action. When we have done our individual duty, that is as good as having extinguished the whole of the fire. In appearance, it is still burning, but we may rest assured that it has been put out. This is all that I have found as a result of my quest of Truth. If it is incorrect, practice of and insistence on Truth (**Satyagraha**) will be impossible. We can only insist upon what is possible. It is no use pining after the air of the mountains on the moon, as it is beyond our reach. The same is true of our duty. Every one of us has, in fact, discovered where his duty lies, for he has not to go far in order to find it. He must only dispose of the refuse in front of him. When he has disposed of it, he will discover more refuse and deal with it. The task of disposing of refuse may be incomplete when life comes to an end. But life never has an end. It is only the body that ends and its end need not worry us. And if life is endless, we should not be tired if the refuse to be disposed of also seems to be endless. The tailor's son will sew clothes till he lives, as they say in Gujarati. If he draws his last breath, needle in hand, he has discharged his duty in the fullest measure.[17]

No Self-Indulgence in Service

IF the body serves but the mind is absent, our service can bear no fruit at all. There can be no self-indulgence in service. The fragrance of your service will spread itself. A servant does not ask to become leader. He expects no service from others. He is satisfied with what he gets and has no complaints at all. He has only the right to serve. What matters if he does not get food or shelter in return?

It is God's grace that there are undistressed persons even in the areas of distress. When all are in distress, who can serve the nurses ? So, we must fend for ourselves when we go out to serve. We must not rely on others, but should be thankful to them for such help as they can afford to give.[18]

Do Not Say : ' I Do It '

WHEN you serve, do not give yourself up to spiritual pride and say : "I do it." The service of the proud is nothing worth. The **Gita** is there to teach us that we do nothing, that we can do nothing. We are only the instruments of God's Will.* What is the difference between a watch and a human being ? A watch does not work by itself; it is set going by a man. In the same way, we do not move, we do not act by ourselves. The power that moves us is God. Just as a watch stops when its wound-up spring has run out, so also when our spring is done, our cart comes to a dead halt. While it is still on the move, we feel that a certain freedom of action is granted to us. Let us use that freedom to learn and do the will of the Great Carpenter.[19]

The Art of Living

IT is not literacy or learning which makes a man, but education for real life. What does it matter if we knew everything, but did not know how to live in brotherliness with our neighbours ?

If some people have committed grievous mistakes in their dealings with their neighbours, they should repent and ask the pardon of God. If He grants it but the world does not, even then it does not matter to a man who has learnt to depend on God; such punishment nobly borne serves to elevate a man. In a book of sayings of the Prophet, I have found that a man should never leave an error uncorrected. If he did, he would be hauled up on the Day of Judgment and find no favour in the eyes of God.

---

* "When you render yourself a willing instrument of service, inexpressible joy is the reward."

—*My Dear Child* : p. 43.

It is not enough that we acquire the art of reading, writing, etc., but it is necessary that we should learn the art of living on friendly terms with neighbours. We should rescue the women-folk, who form half our numbers, from the thraldom of ignorance and superstition. Men should live in cc-operation and work for the common good. For this, they should not look up to political parties for direction, but to their own souls or God.[20]

Service of One's Neighbours

A MAN'S first duty is to his neighbour. Our capacity for service has obvious limits. We can serve even our neighbour with some difficulty. If every one of us duly performed his duty to his neighbour, no one in the world who needed assistance would be left unattended. Therefore, one who serves his neighbour serves all the world. Indeed, it is the only way open to us of serving the world. One, to whom the whole world is as his family, should have the power of serving the universe without moving from his place. He can exercise this power only through service rendered to his neighbour.

Tolstoy goes further and says that at present we are riding on other people's backs; it is enough only if we get down. This is another way of putting the same thing. No one can serve others without serving himself. And whoever tries to achieve his private ends without serving others, harms himself as well as the world at large. The reason is obvious. All living beings are members one of another, so that a person's every act has a beneficial or harmful influence on the whole world. We cannot see this, near-sighted as we are. The influence of a single act of an individual on the world may be negligible. But that influence is there all the same, and an awareness of this truth should make us realize our responsibility.

In trying to serve the world, one does not serve the world and fails to serve even the neighbour. In serving the neighbour, one, in effect, serves the world. Only he who has performed his duty to his neighbour has the right to say : ' All are akin to me.'*   But if a person says : ' All are akin to me' and, neglecting his neighbour gives himself up to self-indulgence, he lives to himself alone.[21]

Pure service of our neighbours can never, from its very nature, result in disservice to those who are far away, but rather the contrary. 'As with the individual, so with the universe' is an unfailing principle, which we would do well to lay to heart. On the other hand, a man who allows himself to be lured by ' the distant scene,' runs to the ends of the earth for service, is not only foiled in his ambition, but also fails in his duty towards his neighbours. Take a concrete instance. In the particular place where I live, I have certain persons as my neighbours, some relations and dependants. Naturally, they all feel, as they have a right to, that they have a claim on me, and look to me for help and support. Suppose now I leave them all at once, and set out to serve people in a distant place. My decision would throw my little world of neighbours and dependants out of gear, while my gratuitous knight-errantry would, more likely than not, disturb the atmosphere in the new place.

It is not difficut to multiply such instances. That is why the **Gita** says : 'It is best to die performing one's own duty or **Swadharma**; **Paradharma** or another's duty is fraught with danger.'

There may arise occasions, when a votary may be called upon to sacrifice his family at the altar of universal service. Such an act of willing immolation will then constitute the highest service rendered to the family. 'Whosoever saveth his life shall lose it, and whosoever loseth his life for the Lord's sake shall find it' holds good for the family group

---

* "The safest rule of conduct is to claim kinship when we want to do service, and not to insist on kinship when we want to assert a right."

—*Young India* : December 8, 1927.

no less than for the individual. Take another instance. Supposing, there is an outbreak of plague in my village, and in trying to serve the victims of the epidemic, I, my wife and children and all the rest of my family are wiped out of existence; then, in inducing those dearest and nearest to join me, I will not have acted as the destroyer of my family; but, on the contrary, as its truest friend.[22]

Self-Sacrifice

A MAN, whose spirit of sacrifice does not go beyond his own community, becomes selfish himself and also makes his community selfish. In my opinion, the logical conclusion of self-sacrifice is that the individual sacrifices himself for the community, the community sacrifices itself for the district, the district for the province, the province for the nation and the nation for the world. A drop torn from the ocean perishes without doing any good. If it remains a part of the ocean, it shares the glory of carrying on its bosom a fleet of mighty ships.[23]

Duties to self, to the family, to the country and to the world are not independent of one another. One cannot do good to the country by injuring himself or his family. Similarly, one cannot serve the country by injuring the world at large. In the final analysis, we must die that the family may live; the family must die that the country may live; and the country must die that the world may live. But only pure things can be offered in sacrifice. Therefore, self-purification is the first step. When the heart is pure, we at once realize what is our duty at every moment.[24]

Definition of a Pure Sacrifice

IT is not the thoughtless annihilation of the moth in the flame. Sacrifice to be effective must be backed by the uttermost external and internal purity. There is nothing that such sacrifice cannot achieve. Without the requisite purity, sacrifice is no better than a desperate self-annihilation devoid of any merit. Sacrifice must further be willing, and it should be made in the faith and hope, without a trace of hatred or ill-will in the heart.[25]

Law of Service

TO proceed a little further, sacrifice means laying down one's life so that others may live. Let us suffer, so that others may be happy; and the highest service and the highest love is wherein man lays down his life for his fellowmen. That highest love is thus **Ahimsa,** which is the highest service. There is an eternal struggle between life and death, but the sum total of life and death does not mean extinction but life. For, life persists in spite of death. We have an ocular demonstration, positive proof of the unquestioned sovereignty of **Ahimsa,** and this triumph of **Ahimsa** is possible through sacrifice. There is thus no higher law than the Law of **Yajna,** the Law of Service. Even for those whom you love most, you may not hate anyone else. If you do, it will not be love or service, but infatuation.[26]

Service of the Universe

THE world cannot subsist for a single moment without **Yajna.*** Therefore the **Gita,** after having dealt with true wisdom in the Second Chapter, takes up in the Third the means of attaining it, and declares in so many words, that **Yajna** came with the Creation itself. This body, therefore, has been given us only in order that we may serve all Creation with it. And, therefore, says the **Gita,** he who eats without offering **Yajna** eats stolen food. Every single act of one, who would live a life of purity, should be in the nature of **Yajna. Yajna** having come to us with our birth, we are debtors all our lives, and thus for ever bound to serve the universe. And even as a bondslave receives food, clothing and so on from the master whom he serves, so should we

---

* "*Yajna* means an act directed to the welfare of others, done without desiring any return for it, whether of a temporal or spiritual nature. 'Act' here must be taken in its widest sense, and includes thought and word, as well as deed. 'Others' embraces not only humanity, but all life."

—*From Yeravda Mandir* : Chap. XIV.

gratefully accept such gifts as may be assigned to us by the Lord of the Universe. What we receive must be called a gift, for, as debtors, we are entitled to no consideration for the discharge of our obligations. Therefore, we may not blame the Master if we fail to get it. Our body is His, to be cherished or cast away according to His will. This is not a matter for complaint or even pity; on the contrary, it is natural and even a pleasant and desirable state, if only we realize our proper place in God's scheme. We do indeed need strong faith, if we would experience this supreme bliss. 'Do not worry in the least about yourself, leave all worry to God',—this appears to be the commandment in all religions.

This need not frighten anyone. He, who devotes himself to service with a clear conscience, will day by day grasp the necessity for it in greater measure, and will continually grow richer in faith. The path of service can hardly be trodden by one who is not prepared to renounce self-interest, and to recognize the conditions of his birth. Consciously or unconsciously, every one of us does render some service or other. If we cultivate the habit of doing this service deliberately, our desire for service will steadily grow stronger, and will make not only for our own happiness but that of the world at large.[27]

Duty of Renunciation

YAJNA is duty to be performed, or service to be rendered, all the twenty-four hours of the day. To serve without desire is to favour not others but ourselves, even as in discharging a debt we serve only ourselves, lighten our burden and fulfil our duty. Again, not only the good, but all of us are bound to place our resources at the disposal of humanity. And if such is the law, as evidently it is, indulgence ceases to hold a place in life and gives way to renunciation. The duty of renunciation differentiates mankind from the beast.

Some object, that life thus understood becomes dull and devoid of art, and leaves no room for the householder. But renunciation here does not mean abandoning the world and retiring into the forest. The spirit of renunciation should rule all the activities of life. A householder does not cease to be one, if he regards life as a duty rather than as an indulgence. A merchant, who operates in the sacrificial spirit, will have crores passing through his hands; but he will, if he follows the law, use his abilities for service. He will, therefore, not cheat or speculate, will lead a simple life, will not injure a living soul and will lose millions rather than harm anybody. Let no one run away with the idea that this type of merchant exists only in my imagination. Fortunately for the world, it does exist in the West as well as in the East. It is true such merchants may be counted on one's fingers' ends, but the type ceases to be immaginary, as soon as even one living specimen can be found to answer to it.

A life of sacrifice is the pinnacle of art, and is full of true joy. **Yajna** is not **Yajna** if one feels it to be burdensome or annoying. Self-indulgence leads to destruction, and renunciation to immortality. Joy has no independent existence. It depends upon our attitude to life. One man will enjoy theatrical scenery, another the ever new scenes which unfold themselves in the sky. Joy, therefore, is a matter of individual and national education. We shall delight in things which we have been taught to delight in as children. And illustrations can be easily cited of different national tastes.

One who would serve will not waste a thought upon his own comforts, which he leaves to be attended to or neglected by his Master on High. He will not, therefore, encumber himself with everything that comes his way; he will take only what he strictly needs and leave the rest. He will be calm, free from anger and unruffled in mind, even if he finds himself inconvenienced. His service, like virtue, is its own reward, and he will rest content with it.

Again, one dare not be negligent in service, or be behind-hand with it. He, who thinks that he must be diligent only in his personal business, and unpaid public business may be done in any way and at any time he chooses, has still to learn the very rudiments of the Science of Sacrifice. Voluntary service of others demands the best of which one is capable, and must take precedence over service of self. In fact, the pure devotee consecrates himself to the service of humanity without any reservation whatever.[28]

CHAPTER XII

ON CONFESSION OF ERRORS

Make a Clean Confession

IF you want really to serve, you must keep your bodies and minds pure so as to make of yourselves a fit instrument for carrying out His work. If you awake every morning with His name on your lips and invoke His aid to help you in your struggles during the day and at night-time before retiring, take off the day's failures and lapses, make a confession of them to your Maker and do a sincere penance for them,—the only fitting penance for a lapse is to make a firm resolve not to allow it to happen again,—you will thereby build, as it were, a solid wall of protection round you and gradually temptations will cease to assail you.[1]

Anyone who has committed a sin should make a clean confession to God, and then depend upon God for whatever He may choose to do. Truly religious men, who make a confession to God, do not repeat their errors.[2]

A full and candid admission of one's mistake should make one proof against its repetition. A full realization of one's mistake is also the highest form of expiation.[3]

Self-Purification is Penance

Q. Is not the realization of one's error and the resolve never to repeat it a penance in itself? Is any further penance necessary?

A. Realization of an error, which amounts to a fixed resolve never to repeat it, is enough penance.* One casts

---

* "We learn through mistakes. But where there is consciousness of mistakes, readiness to mend is sufficient penance and antidote in a majority of cases."

—*Bapu's Letters to Mira* : p. 20.

away his evil habits as a snake casts off his skin, and thus purifies himself. Such self-purification is itself complete penance. But he who gets into the habit of committing errors cannot easily shed it. For all such, penance, in its accepted sense, if undertaken with discrimination, is likely to be a great help.[4]

Effects of Real Penances

IT is my firm belief that all real penances produce unseen but sure effects. The man who performs such penances throws himself wholly and solely on God. He does not undertake such a penance lightly, never in anger, and not certainly with a view to winning any advantage for himself. Then, it must not be against an opponent with whom there is no bond of affection. Then, it presupposes personal purity and a living belief in Non-violence and Truth. Obviously, there can be no room for pride in such penances.[5]

Confession of Error

CONFESSION of error is like a broom that sweeps away dirt and leaves the surface cleaner than before.[6]

We should make a frank confession of error in the past and promise to avoid it in future. He who tries to hide his mistakes can never rectify them. I myself am a votary of Truth. Even when I practised law, I told my clients to tell me the truth if they wanted me to take up their case. I would not plead for a false case. The result was that only true and **bona fide** cases were brought to me. I have long ceased to practise law and have even been struck off the rolls of the Bar register for the offence of sedition. But I continue to follow the same principle.[7]

There is no defeat in the confession of one's error. The confession itself is a victory.[8]

There can never be Truth where there is no courage. To do wrong is sin; but to hide the wrong is a greater sin. He who admits his misdeed with a pure heart, has his sin washed off, and he can travel once more by the straight path. But he who hides his misdeed out of a false sense of shame, falls into a deeper pit. We have seen this to be true every time, and hence I request all to avoid a false sense of shame. If you have done wrong, whether knowingly or unknowingly, announce it at once and make a resolve not to do it again.[9]

Q. How can a person ever be eager to admit a fault ? Will he not be ashamed of doing so ? Still, why do you say that he should not be so ashamed ?

A. A fault is a bad thing ; therefore, we should be ashamed of it. But to admit and ask pardon for a fault is a good thing ; therefore, we should not feel shame in doing so. To ask pardon for a fault implies a determination not to default any more. Is such determination something to be ashamed of ? There can be no comparison between Truth and Non-violence. But if such comparison must be instituted, I would say that Truth is superior even to Non-violence. For, untruth is tantamount to violence. The lover of Truth is bound to make a discovery of Non-violence sooner or later.[10]

To Err is Human

TO err is human. By confessing we convert our mistakes into stepping stones for advance. On the contrary, a person who tries to hide his mistakes becomes a living fraud and sinks down. Man is neither brute nor God, but a creature of God striving to realize his Divinity. Repentance and self-purification are the means. The moment we repent and ask God for forgiveness for our lapse, we are purged of our sin and new life begins for us. True repentance is an essential prerequisite of prayer. Prayer is not mere lip service. It must express itself through action.

I believe in confessing one's mistakes and correcting them. Such confession strengthens one and purifies the soul.[11]

To err is human, and to mend is also human. But to know that you err and still not to mend, is less than human. For, brutes don't err. But ' less than human ' is not the word. To err is human, not to err is Divine. To try to mend is human, but not to try to mend is devilish. That is the proper word.[12]

To err—even grievously—is human. But it is human only if there is a determination to mend the error and not to repeat it. The error will be forgotten if the promise is fully redeemed.[13]

Importance of Confession

I HAVE ever followed the maxim, that one should not let the sun go down upon one's error without confessing it. No mortal is proof against error. Danger consists in conceal-ing one's error, in adding untruth to it in order to gloss it over. When a boil becomes septic, you press out the poison and it subsides. But should the poison spread inward, it would spell certain death. Years ago, in Sabarmati **Ashram,** we had several cases of small-pox. All those in which the eruption came out escaped. But in one case it did not come out, the whole body became red and inflamed and the poor patient died. Even so, it is with error and sin. To con-fess an error or sin as soon as it is discovered, is to purge it out.

I draw no distinction between error and sin. If a man commits a **bona fide** mistake and confesses it with a contrite heart before his Maker, the merciful Maker sterilizes it of all harm.* Throughout my long life, I do not remember a single instance of anybody having suffered harm as a result of **bona fide** mistakes.

There is a saying in English that there is none so fallen but can redeem himself, if only he has the will. We have the promise that no matter how far gone in sin the sinner may be, God will forgive him, if he confesses his sin and repents of it even with his last breath. I believe in future life and in the continuity of **Karma** through successive births.

---

* "He who atones for sins never calculates ; he pours out the whole essence of his contrite heart."

—*Harijan* : June 3, 1939.

What we sow here, we must reap elsewhere—there is no escape. But if one repents even on one's death-bed, the repentance will burn away sin and sterilize it of consequences.[14]

Unintended Errors

I BELIEVE that if in spite of the best of intentions one is led into committing mistakes, they do not really result in harm to the world or, for the matter of that, any individual. God always saves the world from the consequences of unintended errors of man who lives in fear of Him. In the final analysis, a man is guided in his conduct by his own inner promptings, though the example of others might sometimes **seem** to guide him. Indeed, what may appear to be an obvious error to one may appear to another as pure wisdom. He cannot help himself even if he is under a hallucination. Truly has Tulsidas said :

"Even though there never is silver in mother-of-pearl nor water in the sunbeams, while the illusion of silver in the shining shell or that of water in the beams lasts, no power on earth can shake the deluded man free from the spell."

Even so must it be with men like me who, it may be, are labouring under a great hallucination. Surely, God will pardon them and the world should bear with them. Truth will assert itself in the end.[15]

A Man of Truth

A MAN of Truth must ever be confident, if he has also equal need to be diffident. His devotion to Truth demands the fullest confidence. His consciousness of the fallibility of human nature must make him humble and, therefore, ever ready to retrace his steps immediately he discovers his error. It makes no difference to his confidence that he has previously made Himalayan blunders. His confession and penance make him, if anything, stronger for future action.

Discovery of errors makes the votary of Truth more cautious of believing things and forming conclusions ; but once he has made up his mind, his confidence must remain unshaken. His errors may result in men's reliance upon his judgments being shaken, but he must not doubt the truth of his position once he has come to a conclusion.[16]

CHAPTER XIII

ON BEING HUMBLE

What True Humility Means

A LIFE of service must be one of humility. He, who would sacrifice his life for others has hardly time to reserve for himself a place in the sun. Inertia must not be mistaken for humility, as it has been in Hinduism. True humility means most strenuous and constant endeavour, entirely directed towards the service of humanity. God is continuously in action without resting for a single moment. If we would serve Him or become one with Him, our activity must be as unwearied as His. There may be momentary rest in store for the drop which is separated from the ocean, but not for the drop in the ocean which knows no rest. The same is the case with ourselves. As soon as we become one with the ocean in the shape of God, there is no more rest for us, nor indeed do we need rest any longer. Our very sleep is action. For, we sleep with the thought of God in our hearts. This restlessness constitutes true rest. This never-ceasing agitation holds the key to peace ineffable. This supreme state of total surrender is difficult to describe, but not beyond the bounds of human experience. It has been attained by many dedicated souls and may be attained by ourselves as well.[1]

On Giving Up Pride

OUR joy must lie in our devotion to duty, and not in the success of our efforts or in the favourableness of circumstances. Narsinha Mehta has said : ' If man had the power to do everything, no one would be unhappy, for he would destroy his enemies and allow only friends to live '. But man is a lowly creature. He becomes great only when he gives up pride and becomes one with God. A drop of the ocean, if separated from it, serves no useful purpose ; but remaining in the ocean, it shares in bearing on its bosom the heavy burden of a huge steamer. In the same way, if we learn to be one with the world and God, we may be said to be bearing the burden of the world. But in such a state, the ' I ' or ' You ' is abandoned, and only ' He ' remains.[2]

Take water, which in its solid state remains on the earth ; it cannot ascend until it is rarefied into steam. But once it is rarified into steam, it rises up in the sky where at last it is transformed into the clouds which drop down in the form of rain and fructify and bless the earth. We are like water, we have to strive so to rarefy ourselves that all the ego in us perishes and we merge in the Infinite to the eternal good of all.[3]

He who thinks that he knows, knows nothing. He who thinks that he knows nothing, acquires knowledge in God's good time. Even Almighty God cannot pour a single drop of water into a pitcher that is full to the brim. We have, therefore, every day to stand before God as beggars with empty hands.[4]

' Judge Not Lest You Be Judged '

' JUDGE not lest you be judged '. Its latter part asks us to beware of falling into the same error ourselves. We must not be haughty in dealing with the world. ' Let the world say or do what it likes ' is a thought which we must not permit to enter our minds. We are humble before the world. Even when we are sure we are on the right path, we do not punish the world or sit in judgment over it. On the other hand, we suffer the world's punishment and bow to its judgment. This is humility or **Ahimsa.**

One need not cultivate haughtiness or incivility in order to stand up against the world. Jesus faced the world and so did Buddha, and Prahlad. But they were all the very picture of humility. The essential requisites are self-confidence and faith in God. Those who opposed the world in their pride have collapsed at last.

The power to stand alone till the end cannot be developed without extreme humility. Without this power, a man is nothing worth. Many who pass as brave people have never had their bravery put to the test.[5]

Be Humble

KABIR, in his homely telling way, has described the treasures of the humble. It is not he that exalteth himself, but he that humbleth himself that shall see God, says Kabir. We have to be humble like the ant and not proud like the elephant.

"Only he who humbleth himself will find the Lord.

It is no use your going to the weaver with coarse yarn, and asking for fine cloth from him.

Hard earth is no use to the potter, unless he beats it into very fine powder for clay. Then and then only can it be fit for the wheel.

An elephant will try in vain to pick up the grains of sugar scattered in grains of sand. But an ant will easily pick them up. Humble thyself, therefore.

For, he who exalteth himself shall be crushed. But says Kabir, he who humbleth himself shall find God."[6]

God Triumphs, Never We

THOSE who cultivate Truth, **Ahimsa, Brahmacharya,** must be humble. Truth without humility would be an arrogant caricature. He who wants to practise Truth knows how hard it is. The world may applaud his so-called triumphs. Little does the world know his falls. A truthful man is a chastened being. He has need to be humble. A man who wants to love the whole world, including one who calls himself his enemy, knows how impossible it is to do so in his own strength. He must be as mere dust before he can understand the elements of **Ahimsa.** He is nothing if he does not daily grow in humility as he grows in love. A man who would have his eye single, who would regard every woman as his blood-sister or mother, has to be less than dust. He stands on the brink of a precipice. The slightest turn of the head brings him down. He dare not whisper his virtue to his very own. For, he knows not what the next moment has in store for him. For him, ' pride goeth before destruction and haughtiness before a fall '. Well has the **Gita** said : ' Passions subside in a fasting man, not the desire for them. The desire goes only when man sees God face to face.' And no one can see God face to face who has aught of the ' I ' in him. He must become a cypher, if he would see God. Who shall dare say in this storm-tossed universe ; ' I have won ' ? God triumphs in us, never we.[7]

Humility Cannot Remain Hidden

HUMILITY does not lend itself to being deliberately practised. It is, however, an indispensable test of **Ahimsa.** In one, who has **Ahimsa** in him, it becomes part of his very nature.

Truth can be cultivated as well as love. But to culti-vate humility is tantamount to cultivating hypocrisy. Humility must not be here confounded with mere manners or etiquette. One man will sometimes prostrate himself before another, although his heart is full of bitterness against the latter. This is not humility, but cunning. A man may repeat **Ramanama,** or tell his beads all the day long, and move in society like a sage ; but if he is selfish at heart, he is not meek but only hypocritical.

A humble person is not himself conscious of his humi-lity. Truth and the like, perhaps, admit of measurement, but not humility. Inborn humility can never remain hidden, and yet the possessor is unaware of its existence. The story of Vasishtha and Vishvamitra furnishes a very good case in point. Humility should make the possessor **realize** that he is as nothing. Directly one imagines oneself to be some-thing, there is egotism. If a man who keeps observances,*

---

* The reference is to 11 Ashram Observances, *viz.* (1) Truth, (2) Non-violence, (3) *Brahmacharya,* (4) Control of the Palate, (5) Non-stealing, (6) Non-possession (7) Fearlessness, (8) Re-moval of Untouchability, (9) Bread-Labour, (10) Equality of Reli-gions, (11) *Swadeshi.*

who is proud of keeping them, will lose much if not all of their value. And a man who is proud of his virtue often becomes a curse to society. Society will not appreciate it, and he himself will fail to reap any benefit from it. Only a little thought will suffice to convince us that all creatures are nothing more than a mere atom in this universe. What are a hundred years in Eternity? But if we shatter the chains of egotism, and melt into the ocean of humanity, we share its dignity. To feel that we are something is to set up a barrier between God and ourselves; to cease feeling that we are something is to become one with God. A drop in the ocean partakes of the greatness of its parent, although it is unconscious of it; but it is dried up as soon as it enters upon an existence independent of the ocean. We do not exaggerate when we say that life on earth is a mere bubble.[8]

CHAPTER XIV

ON BIRTH AND DEATH

This Earthly Existence of Ours

THIS earthly existence is no more permanent than that of the moths we see every night dancing round lights for a few minutes and then being destroyed. This earthly existence of ours is more brittle than the glass bangles that ladies wear. You can keep glass bangles for thousands of years, if you treasure them in a chest and let them remain untouched. But this earthly existence is so fickle that it may be wiped out in the twinkling of an eye. Therefore, whilst we have yet breathing time, let us get rid of the distinctions of high and low, purify our hearts, and be ready to face our Maker when an earthquake or some natural calamity or death in the ordinary course overtakes us.[1]

So long as we wear this vesture of clay, let us keep it clean, pure and healthy ; and when we have to cast it off, let us discard it without any regret. It was given to us for use. Let the Giver take it away when He pleases. We have to use it for service only, and not for enjoyment.

The human body is less durable even than a glass bangle, which, if well preserved, may continue to exist for hundreds of years. But our bodies, no matter how carefully preserved, cannot last beyond a certain period, and may be destroyed at any time during that period. We may not put our trust in them.[2]

Why Rejoice in a Birth and Lament a Death ?

WHY should we be upset when children or young men or old men die ? Not a moment passes when some one is not born or is not dead in this world. We should feel the stupidity of rejoicing in a birth and lamenting a death.

Those who believe in the soul—and what Hindu, Mussalman or Parsi is there who does not ?—know that the soul never dies. The souls of the living as well as of the dead are all one. The eternal processes of creation and destruction are going on ceaselessly. There is nothing in it for which we might give ourselves up to joy or sorrow. Even if we extend the idea of relationship only to our countrymen and take all the births in the country as taking place in our own family, how many births shall we celebrate ? If we weep for all the deaths in our country, the tears in our eyes would never dry. This train of thought should help us to get rid of all fear of death.

India, they say, is a nation of philosophers ; and we have not been unwilling to appropriate the compliment. Still, hardly any other nation becomes so helpless in the face of death as we do. And in India again, no other community perhaps betrays so much of this helplessness as the Hindus. A single birth is enough for us to be beside ourselves with ludicrous joyfulness. A death makes us indulge in orgies of loud lamentation, which condemn the neighbourhood to sleeplessness for the night. We must perfectly renounce this unseemly fright.[3]

People die only to be born again. Sorrow, therefore, is entirely uncalled for. One who has not mastered the art of standing alone would be upset by external changes. But only they can approach the God of Truth, who are fit to stand alone.[4]

Death as a Deliverance

IN Hindu households, there is too much and unseemly weeping and gnashing of teeth though our religious literature strictly forbids weeping over death. In many places, weeping over the dead has become the fashion and it is simulated where it is not spontaneous. It is a barbarous Godless custom and should be prohibited. Those who have faith in God should welcome death as a deliverance. It is a change as certain as youth and old age, and no more to be deplored than latter.[5]

As Hindus we ought to be the least affected by the thought of death, since from the very cradle we are brought up on the doctrines of the immortality of the spirit and the transitoriness of the body.[6]

Only a Big Change in Life

I BELIEVE that I have an unflinching faith in God. For many years I have accorded intellectual assent to the proposition that death is only a big change in life and nothing more, and should be welcome whenever it arrives. I have deliberately made a supreme attempt to cast out from my heart all fear whatsoever, including the fear of death. Still, I remember occasions in my life when I have not rejoiced at the thought of approaching death, as one might rejoice at the prospect of meeting a long lost friend. Thus, man often remains weak notwithstanding all his efforts to be strong, and knowledge, which stops at the head and does not penetrate into the heart, is of but little use in the critical times of living experience. Then again, the strength of the spirit within mostly evaporates when a person gets and accepts support from outside.[7]

The Soul is Immortal

THE soul is immortal, unchangeable and immanent. It does not perish with the physical body, but journeys on from one mortal frame to another till it completely emancipates itself from earthly bondage. The truth of it has been attested to by the experience of countless sages and seers, and can be realized by anyone who may wish to, even today.[8]

Our scriptures tell us that childhood, old age and death are incident only to this perishable body of ours, and that man's spirit is eternal and immortal. That being so, why should we fear death ? And where there is no fear of death, there can be no sorrow over it either.[9]

Death is a true friend. It is only our ignorance that causes us grief. Spirit was yesterday, is today and will remain tomorrow. The body, of course, must die.[10]

I believe in the immortality of the soul. I would like to give the analogy of ocean. The ocean is composed of drops of water ; each drop is an entity and yet it is part of the whole, ' the one and the many '. In this ocean of life, we are all little drops. My doctrine means that I must identify myself with life, with everything that lives, that I must share the majesty of life in the presence of God. The sum total of this life is God.[11]

Twice Blessed for a Warrior

DEATH is at any time blessed, but it is twice blessed for a warrior who dies for his cause, i.e., Truth. Death is no fiend, he is the truest of friends. He delivers us from agony. He helps us against ourselves. He ever gives us new chances, new hopes. He is, like sleep, a sweet restorer. Yet, it is customary to mourn when a friend dies. The custom has no operation when the death is that of a martyr.[12]

Every brave man welcomes death (of a hero) whenever it comes to him. He greets it as a friend. But let no one, therefore, invite or hanker after such a death, let no one desire that some one else should be in the wrong and err against God and man, so that he might become a martyr. It is wrong to wish anyone to go astray. Let us all be brave enough to die the death of a martyr, but let no one lust for martyrdom.[13]

Phases of the Same Thing

IT is as clear to me as daylight that life and death are but phases of the same thing, the reverse and obverse of the same coin. In fact, tribulation and death seem to me to present a phase far richer than happiness or life. What is life worth without trials and tribulation, which are the salt of life ? The history of mankind would have been a blank sheet without these individuals. What is **Ramayana** but a record of the trials, privations and penances of Rama and Sita ? The life of Rama, after the recovery of Sita, full of happiness as it was, does not occupy even a hundredth part of the epic. I want you all to treasure death and suffering more than life and to appreciate their cleansing and purifying character.[14]

Suffering, cheerfully endured, ceases to be suffering and is transmuted into an ineffable joy. The man who flies from suffering is the victim of endless tribulation before it has come to him, and is half dead when it does come. But one, who is cheerfully ready for anything and everything that comes, escapes all pain ; his cheerfulness acts as an anaesthetic.[15]

Terror of Terrors

DEATH continues to haunt man as the terror of terrors.* Whilst we have much in our literature that teaches us to be indifferent to death, there is also much that inculcates in us a paralysing fear of death. In these times, when we wish to contemplate death in the cause of the country as a matter of joy and honour, the following extract sent by a friend from Lecky's **History of European Morals** will be of interest :

> " There was much difference of opinion and of certitude in the judgments of the ancient philosophers (the Stoics) concerning the future destinies of the Soul, but they were un-animous in regarding death simply as a natural rest, and in attributing the terrors that were connected with it to a diseased imagination. Death, they said, is the only evil that does not afflict us when present. While we are, death is not ; when death has come, we are not. It is a false belief that it only follows, it also precedes life. It is to be as we were

---

* "To the God-fearing, death has no terror. It is a joyful sleep to be followed by a waking that would be all the more refreshing for the long sleep."

before we were born. The candle which has been extinguished is in the same condition as before it was lit, and the dead man as the man unborn. Death is the end of all sorrow. It either secures happiness or ends suffering. It frees the slave from his cruel master, opens the prison door, calms the qualms of pain, closes the struggle of poverty. It is the last and best boon of Nature, for it frees man from all his cares. It is, at worst, but the close of a banquet we have enjoyed. Whether it be desired or whether it be shunned, it is no curse and no evil, but simply the resolution of our being into its primitive elements, the Law of our Nature to which it is our duty cheerfully to conform."

*   *   *

" Death, according to Socrates, either extinguishes life or emancipates it from the thraldom of the body. Even in the first case, it is a blessing—in the last, it is the greatest of boons. ' Accustom yourself,' said Epicures, ' to the thought that death is indifferent ; for, all good, all evil consist in feeling ; and what is death but the privation of feeling ? ' ' Souls either remain after death,' says Cicero, ' or they perish in death. If they remain, they are happy ; if they perish, they are not wretched.' Seneca exhorts his friend to think, ' If the dead have any sensations, then my brother, let loose as it were from a life-long prison and at last enjoying his liberty, looks down from a loftier height on the wonders of Nature and on all the deeds of men, and sees more clearly those Divine things which he has so long sought in vain to understand. But why should I be afflicted for one who is either happy or is nothing ? To lament the fate of one who is happy is envy, to lament the fate of a nonentity is madness.' "[16]

Communication with Spirits

I NEVER receive communications from the spirits of the dead. I have no evidence warranting a disbelief in the possibility of such communications. But I do strongly disapprove of the practice of holding or attempting to hold such communications. They are often deceptive and are products of imagination. The practice is harmful both to the medium and the spirits, assuming the possibility of such communications. It attracts and ties to the earth the spirit so invoked, whereas its effort should be to detach itself from the earth, and rise higher. A spirit is not necessarily purer because it is disembodied. It takes with it most of the frailties to which it was liable when on earth. Information or advice, therefore, given by it need not be true or sound. That the spirit likes communications with those on earth is no matter for pleasure. On the contrary, it should be weaned from such unlawful attachment. So much for the harm done to the spirits.

As for the medium, it is a matter of positive knowledge with me that all those within my experience have been deranged or weak-brained and disabled for practical work, whilst they were holding or thought they were holding such communications. I can recall no friend of mine who, having held such communication, had benefited in any way.[17]

Predestination

Q. Are the time, place and manner of death predestined by the Almighty for each individual? If so, why worry even if we are ill?

A. I do not know whether time, place and the manner of death are predestined. All I do know is that 'not a blade of grass moves but by His will'. This, too, I know hazily. What is hazy today will be clear tomorrow or the day after by prayerful waiting. Let this, however, be quite clear. The Almighty is not a person like us. He or It is the greatest living Force or Law in the world. Accordingly, He does not act by caprice, nor does that Law admit of any amendment or improvement. His will is fixed and changeless, everything else changes every second. Surely, it does not follow from the Doctrine of Predestination that we may not 'worry' in the care of ourselves even if we are ill. Indifference to illness is a crime greater than that of falling ill. There is no end to the effort to do better today than yesterday. We have to 'worry' and find out why we are or have become ill. Health, not 'illth', is the Law of Nature. Let us investigate the Law of Nature and obey it, if we will not be ill or, if having fallen ill, will be restored.[18]

I am fatalist enough to believe that no one can put off the hour of death when it has struck. Not the greatest medical assistance available has saved kings and emperors from the jaws of death.[19]

I may not be able to convince others, but I do feel that death is never untimely in the real sense of the term. No one dies before he or she has finished his work in this world.[20]

Death which is an eternal verity, is revolution, as birth and after is slow and steady evolution. Death is as necessary for man's growth as life itself.[21]

Death is a blessing bestowed by the Creator on all life, human and sub-human. The difference lies in the time and the manner. Right conduct is the only right way of life which makes it bearable and even lovely.[22]

Unlawful Peep Beyond

Q. " Ah, Christ ! that it were possible
For one short hour to see
The souls we loved, that they might tell us
What and where they be."

What would you say ?

A. The poet expresses, in the above, the cry of many an anguished heart. Nevertheless, the truly detached mind does not care to know the Beyond. In other words it is wrong to have the desire. Therefore, the following from the well-known hymn of Cardinal Newman represents the reality :

" I do not ask to see the distant scene,
One step enough for me." [23]

Love Death As Well As Life

MAN does not live but to escape death. If he does so, he is advised not to do so. He is advised to learn to love death as well as life, if not more so. A hard saying, harder to act up to, one may say. Every worthy act is difficult. Ascent is always difficult. Descent is easy and often slippery. Life becomes livable only to the extent that death is treated as a friend, never as an enemy. To conquer life's temptations, summon death to your aid. In order to postpone death, a coward surrenders honour, wife, daughter and all. A courageous man prefers death to the surrender of self-respect.[24]

It is foolish to think that by fleeing, one can trick the dread God of Death. Let us treat him as a beneficient Angel rather than as a dread God. We must face and welcome him, whenever he comes.[25]

Man is Born to Die

IF we have a living faith in God, we will realize that it is the mortal body that perishes, never the immortal Spirit within. Man is born to die. Death is the natural corollary to birth. So, whether God sends us natural death or whether we are killed by the assassin's knife, we must go smiling to our end. I, therefore, ask all to pray to God to vouchsafe to us the living faith that enables one to put oneself entirely under His protection without reliance on any outside help, and to remember that He never fails His devotees.[26]

Gitaji proclaims that everyone that is born must die, and everyone that dies must be born again. Everyone comes, repays part of his obligation, and goes his way. I am positive that there is no disease without the existence within oneself of passion. Of course, even the man who is free from passion has also to die, but he drops off, without a disease or even a headache, like a ripe fruit dropping off the tree. I have aspired to and hoped for such a consummation. The hope still abides, but who knows ? The passions are not yet extinct, and freedom from them looks like a far off thing.[27]

Why Fear Death ?

NONE should fear death. Death is inevitable for every human being. But if one dies smiling, one would enter into a new life. The Second Chapter of the **Gita** describes in its ending **shlokas** how the God-fearing man should live and move and have his being. I want you to read, mark, learn and inwardly digest the meaning of every one of those **shlokas.** We will, then, realize what our ideals are and how far short of them we have fallen today.[28]

All must die some day. No one could escape death. Then, why be afraid of it ? In fact, death is a friend which brings deliverance from sufferings.[29]

A man should be free from fear even when he has to sleep in the cemetery on the very first day. It is possible that he will only lose his life. We must prepare ourselves ere to make our beds there and sing Mirabai's hymn : Take thought of nothing except the name of God."

To be afraid of death is like being afraid of discarding an old and worn-out garment. I have often thought of death and have the intellectual conviction that it is sheer ignorance which makes us afraid of death. I am, however, not sure that this conviction has become part and parcel of my spiritual being, I say this in view of my reactions when I see a snake, for instance. And yet I feel that I will acquire the necessary strength to welcome death, whenever and however it comes.

Shocks make in me for still more intense fearlessness of death. Why should the event agitate one ? The grief itself has a selfish touch about it. It is no calamity that my brother is dead, if I am ready to meet death and consider it as the supreme and welcome crisis in life. It is because we fear death so much for ourselves that we shed tears over the death of others. How can I, who know the body to be perishable and the soul to be imperishable, mourn over the separation of body from soul ? But there is a condition attached to a real belief in this beautiful and consoling doctrine. He who believes in it, must not pamper the body but must be its ruler. He must regulate his wants so as to make it serve the Dweller within. Not to grieve over the death of others is to accept a state almost of perpetual grief. For, this connection between body and soul is itself grievous.[30]

Cycle of Birth and Death

BOTH birth and death are two different aspects of one and the same thing. He who is born has to die ; he who dies is born again. Some do get out of this cycle of birth and death ; but, whether in or out of this cycle, one has no reason to feel pleasure or pain due to birth or death.[31]

Birth and death are not two different states, but they are different aspects of the same state. There is as little reason to deplore the one, as there is to be pleased over the other.[32]

We die to live once more, even as we live only to die at last. Life, therefore, is not an occasion for joy, nor is death an occasion for sorrow. But there is one thing needful. We must ascertain our duty in life and continue to discharge it till we die. You know what is your duty either by faith or by conviction. See that you are not remiss in your performance of it.[33]

A Comforting Thought

WHAT a comforting thought it is to think of death whenever it comes, as a wise plan in the economy of Nature ? If we could realize this Law of our Being and be prepared for death as a welcome friend and deliverer, we should cease to engage in the frantic struggle for life. We shall cease to want to live at the cost of other lives, and if contempt of all considerations of humanity. But to philosophize is one thing ; to realize at the required moment the truth of the philosophy is totally another. Such realization is impossible without a due conception of the definite and grave limitations of the body and an abiding faith in God and His unchangeable Law of **Karma**.[34]

The Law of **Karma** is inexorable and impossible of evasion. There is thus hardly any need for God to interfere. He laid down the Law and retired, as it were.[35]

' Working for Our Own Schemes '

THE tallest among us has a perpetual reminder of his nothingness before death, disease, old age, accident, etc. We are living in the midst of death. What is the value of ' working for our own schemes ' when they might be reduced to naught in the twinkling of an eye, or when we may be equally swiftly and unawares taken away from them ? But we may feel strong as a rock, if we could truthfully say ' we work for God and His scheme.' Then, all is as clear as daylight. Then, nothing perishes. All perishing is then only what seems. Death and destruction have then, **but only then,** no reality about them. For, death or destruction is then but a change. An artist destroys his picture for creating a better one. A watch-maker throws away a bad spring to put in new and useful one.[36]

' Death is Rest '

WHEN I am overwhelmed with correspondence betraying in every line fear of death and consequent travesty of **Ahimsa**, it refreshes me to come across the following beautiful dialogue :

" Tzu Kung said to Confucius : ' Master, I am aweary, and would fain have rest.'

" ' In life,' replied the sage, ' there is no rest.'

" Shall I then never have rest ? ' asked the disciple.

" ' You will,' said Confucius. ' Behold the

tombs which lie around; some magnificent, some mean. In one of these, you will find rest ! '

" ' How wonderful is Death ! ' rejoined Tzu Kung. ' The wise man rests, the wordly man is engulfed therein.'

" ' My son,' said Confucius, ' I see that you understand. Other men know life only as a boon ; they do not perceive that it is a bane. They know old age as a stage of weakness ; they do not perceive that it is a state of ease. They know Death only as an abomination ; they do not perceive that it is a state of rest.'

" ' How grand,' cried Yen Txu, ' is the old conception of Death ! The virtuous find rest ; the wicked are engulfed therein. In Death, each reverts to that from which he came. The ancients regarded Death as a return to, and life as an absence from, home. And he, who forgets his home, becomes an outcaste and a byword in his generation.' "

It is not reproduced to defend the infliction of death penalty on any living being or thing. But it is given here to show that death is not a terror in all circumstances, as many contend, and that it may be a deliverance in certain cases, especially when it is not inflicted as a penalty but administered as a healing balm. ' Death is but a sleep and a forgetting, ' says the English poet. Let us not seek to prop virtue by imagining hellish torture after death for vice, and **houris** hereafter as a reward for virtue in this life. If virtue has no attraction in itself, it must be a poor thing to be thrown away on the dung-heap. Nature, I am convinced, is not so cruel as she seems to us, who are so often filled with cruelty ourselves. Both heaven and hell are within us. Life after death there is, but it is not so unlike our present experiences as either to terrify us or make us delirious with joy. ' He is steadfast who rises above joy and sorrow,' says the **Gita.** ' The wise are unaffected either by death or life.' These are but faces of the same coin.[37]

Separation is Only Superficial

THE few days' separation is a preparation for the longer that death brings. In fact, the separation is only superficial. Death brings us nearer. Is not the body a bar if it is also an introduction ?[38]

The more I observe and study things, the more convinced I become that sorrow over separation and death is perhaps the greatest delusion. To realize that it is a delusion is to become free. There is no death, no separation of the substance. And yet the tragedy of it is that, though we love friends for the substance we recognize in them, we deplore the destruction of the insubstantial that covers the substance for the time being. Whereas, real friendship should be used to reach the whole through the fragment.[39]

It is Nature's kindness that we do not remember past births. Where is the good either of knowing in detail the numberless births we have gone through ? Life would be a burden, if we carried such a tremendous load of memories. A wise man deliberately forgets many things, even as a lawyer forgets the cases and their details as soon as they are disposed of. Yes, ' death is but a sleep and a forgetting.'[40]

It is better to leave a body one has outgrown. To wish to see the dearest ones as long as possible in the flesh, is a selfish desire and it comes out of weakness or want of faith in the survival of the soul after the dissolution of the body. The form ever changes, ever perishes, the Informing Spirit neither changes nor perishes. True love consists in transferring itself from the body to the Dweller within, and then necessarily realizing the oneness of all life inhabiting numberless bodies.[41]

Oneness of All Life

SO mother is gone. I read your suppressed grief in every line of your letter. After all we are very human. The ability to suppress is the preliminary to eradication. God give you the strength. So far as mother herself was concerned, it is, as you say, welcome news. Let this death of one whom you loved so, be a means of enriching your faith in the future and in the oneness of all life. If this oneness was not a fact, we would not have been blessed with the capacity to forget the death of dearest ones. Let this death also spur you to greater dedication to service.

*   *   *

I hope you are now quite at peace with yourself and have realized that the loved one lives more truly for the dissolution of the body and renders the love also truer because unselfish, and also because it is transferred to all that lives. Every death of a friend or a relative should enrich universal love.[42]

Great Mysteries

THERE is a splendid passage in Sir James Jean's book: ' Life is a progress towards Death '. Another reading may be : ' Life is a preparation for Death '. And, somehow or other, we quail to think of that inevitable and grand event. It is grand even regarded as a preparation for a better life than the past, as it should be for everyone who tries to live in the fear of God.[43]

' The valiant only taste of death but once ' has a deeper meaning, conveying the perfect truth according to the Hindu conception of salvation. It means freedom from the Wheel of Birth and Death. If the word ' valiant ' may be taken to mean those who are strong in their search after God, they die but once, for they need not be re-born and put on the mortal coil.[44]

All of us are in His hands. It is well if we live and it is equally well if we die. We are born only to die and we die only to be born again. This is all old argument. Yet, it needs to be driven home. Somehow or other, we refuse to welcome death as we welcome birth. We refuse to believe even the evidence of our senses, that we could not possibly have any attachment for the body without the soul, and that we have no evidence whatsoever that the soul perishes with the body.[45]

Both birth and death are great mysteries. If death is not a prelude to another life, the intermediate period is a cruel mockery. We must learn the art of never grieving over death, no matter when and to whom it comes. I suppose that we shall do when we have really learnt to be utterly indifferent to our own, and the indifference will come when we are every moment conscious of having done the task to which we are called. But how shall we know the task? By knowing God's will. How shall we know the will? By prayer and right living. Indeed, prayer should mean right living.[46]

Nothing but a fixed faith that death for the good is a translation to a better state, and for the evil a beneficent escape, can reconcile us to the mystery of death.[47]

'Things Are Not What They Seem'

GOD suffers us to blame Him, to swear at Him and deny Him. We do it all in our ignorance. A very beautiful Sanskrit verse* means:

> " Miseries are not miseries,
>   Nor is happiness truly happiness.
>   True misery consists in forgetting God,
>   True happiness consists in thinking of Him as
>   ever enthroned in our hearts."

And has not an English poet said:

> " Things are not what they seem "?

The fact is if we knew all the laws of God, we should be able to account for the unaccountable. We simply do

---

* " विपदो नैव विपद:
          संपदो नैव संपद:
विपद विस्मरणं विष्णो:
          सर्पंन्नारायण स्मृति: ॥

not know. But we do, or ought to, know that God is wholly good and wholly just. Even our illness may be no misfortune. Life is a state of discipline. We are required to go through the fire of suffering.

I loathe to argue about death. You will say with Job : ' Miserable comforter.' But I do feel that if we would know God, we have got to learn to rejoice in death. When Narasinha Mehta, the first poet-devotee of Gujarat, lost his son, he is said to have joyed over it and exclaimed : ' It is well that this burden is lifted. Now I shall meet God soon.' This is an unhappy rendering of a beautiful musical verse.[48]

An Inevitable Event

THERE ought not to be much sorrow or fuss over an inevitable event. Death is the lot of every created thing, nor need it be considered as a calamity. Death is, in reality, a deliverance.

What the soul does after discarding a body is in each case a matter for surmise, but it is a certainty that the soul does not perish with the body. Let us trust the laws of God or Nature for the rest.

God is never powerless. But His laws are immutable. We do not know them. Nor do we know His will at a given moment. Therefore, we adopt, within bounds, such remedies as may commend themselves to us. Prayer is to the God within. It does not provoke God to change His will ; but it enables us to know His will which is everything.

States before birth and after death are invisible, as the **Gita** affirms and experience confirms. But we can infer from our present state that the condition after death is at least likely to be a second, though modified, edition of the present.

We, the survivors, can certainly help the departed dear ones by weaving into our own lives all that was good in them. For, if they know anything of what happens here, they must be consoled by the knowledge that we are treasuring their memories by adopting what was best in them.[49]

'Thy Will be Done!'

THERE is really only one prayer that we may offer : "Thy will be done." Someone will ask where is the sense in offering such a prayer. The answer is : Prayer should not be understood in a gross sense. We are aware of the presence of God in our heart, and in order to shake off attachment, we for the moment think of God as different from ourselves and pray to Him. That is to say, we do not wish to go where our wayward will may lead us, but where the Lord takes us. We do not know whether it is good to live or to die. Therefore, we should not take delight in living, nor should we tremble at the thought of death. We should be equiminded towards both. This is the ideal. It may be long before we reach it, and only a few of us can attain it. Even then, we must keep it constantly in view, and the more difficult it seems of attainment, the greater should be the effort we put forth.[50]

When One May Commit Suicide

Q. Life for man is a burdensome and painful thing. Is a man entitled to cast it off ?

A. A man who is suffering from an incurable disease and living, thanks to service rendered to him by others, without himself doing anything useful in return, has the right to end his life. To fast unto death would be much better for him than to drown himself, for it tests his firmness and leaves room for him to change his mind. **Locus penitentiae** is essential. But so long as the man can render some service or other, it would be improper for him to end his life. Physical acts are a big and essential part of sacrifice. If, however, a man is incapable of doing anything with his body, mental activity may not be quite infructuous as sacrifice. We can serve even by pure and holy thought, and by good advice given to others. Thinking, on the part of a holy man, is action capable of producing great results.[51]

Right to Dispose of Life

Q. What would you say to the right of man to dispose of his life ? Life as life I hold of very little importance.

A. I think that man has perfect right to dispose of his life under certain circumstances. A co-worker, suffering from leprosy, knowing that his disease was incurable and that his life was as much an agony for those who had to serve him as it was for him, recently decided to end his life by abstaining from food and water. I blessed the idea. I said to him : 'If you really think you can stand the trial, you may do so.' I said this to him, for I knew how difficult it is to die by inches from, say, suddenly killing oneself by drowning or poisoning. And my warning was fully justified, for someone tempted him with the hope that there was one who could cure leprosy, and I now hear that he has resumed eating and put himself under his treatment !

Q. The criterion seems to me to be that if one's mind is completely obscured by pain, the best thing for him would be to seek **Nirvana.** A man may not be ill, but he may be tired of the struggle.

A. No no, my mind rejects this suicide. The criterion is not that one is tired of life, but that one feels that one has become a burden on others and, therefore, wants to leave the world. One does not want to fly from pain, but from having to become an utter burden on others. Otherwise, one suffers greater pain in a violent effort to end one's agony. But supposing I have a cancer, and it is only a question of time for me to pass away, I would even ask my doctor to give me a sleeping draught and thereby have the sleep that knows no waking.[52]

'Will to Live'

Q. It has been said that the 'will to live' is irrational, being born of a deluded attachment to life. Why is then suicide a sin ?

A. The will to live is not irrational. It is also natural. Attachment to life is not a delusion, it is very real. Above all, life has a purpose. To seek to defeat that purpose is a sin. Therefore, suicide is very rightly held to be a sin.[53]

CHAPTER XV

ON PRAYER AND FAITH

What is Prayer?

PRAYER is the key of the morning and the bolt of the evening.[1]

There is no peace without the grace of God, and there is no grace of God without prayer. That is why I ask you all to observe the habit of prayer. Prayer should proceed from the heart.[2]

Prayer is not an old woman's idle amusement. Properly understood and applied, it is the most potent instrument of action. Undoubtedly, prayer requires a living faith in God.[3]

Heartfelt prayer steadies one's nerves, humbles one and clearly shows one the next step.[4]

Empty prayer is as sounding brass or a tinkling cymbal.

We may miss many things in life but not prayer, which implies our co-operation with God and with one another. Prayer should be a bath of purification for the spirit of man. Physical health suffers, if we do not wash our bodies; similarly, the spirit becomes unclean if the heart is not washed with prayer. Please, therefore, never be negligent in prayer.[6]

Writing to a friend on prayer, I came across a beautiful thing from Tennyson which I present to the readers, if perchance I might convert them to a definite belief in the efficacy of prayer. Here is the gem :

"More things are wrought by prayer
Than this world dreams of. Wherefore, let thy voice
Rise like a fountain for me night and day.
For, what are men better than sheep or goats

That nourish a blind life within the brain,
If, knowing God, they lift not hands of prayer
Both for themselves and those who call them friends ?
For, so the whole round earth is every way
Bound by golden chains about the feet of God."[7]

Prayer — The Soul of Religion

I BELIEVE that prayer is the very soul and essence of religion, and, therefore, prayer must be the very core of the life of man, for no man can live without religion. There are some who, in the egotism of their reason, declare that they have nothing to do with religion. But it is like a man saying that he breathes, but that he has no nose.

Whether by reason, or by instinct, or by superstition, man acknowledges some sort of relationship with the Divine. The rankest agnostic or atheist does acknowledge the need of a moral principle, and associates something good with its observance and something bad with its non-observance. Bradlaugh, whose atheism is well known, always insisted on proclaiming his innermost conviction. He had to suffer a lot for thus speaking the truth, but he delighted in it and said that Truth is its own reward. Not that he was quite insensible to the joy resulting from the observance of Truth. This joy, however, is not at all worldly, but springs out of communion with the Divine. That is why I have said that even a man who disowns religion cannot and does not live without religion.

Now, I come to the next thing **viz.,** that prayer is the very core of man's life, as it is the most vital part of religion. Prayer is either petitional or, in its wider sense, is inward communion. In either case, the ultimate result is the same. Even when it is petitional, the petition should be for the cleansing and purification of the soul, for freeing it from the layers of ignorance and darkness that envelop it. He, therefore, who hungers for the awakening of the Divine in him, must fall back on prayer. But prayer is no mere exercise of words or of the ears, it is no mere repetition of empty formula. Any amount of repetition of **Ramanama** is futile, if it fails to stir the soul. It is better in prayer to have a heart without words than words without a heart. It must be in clear response to the spirit which hungers for it. And even as a hungry man relishes a hearty meal, a hungry soul will relish a heartfelt prayer. And I am giving you a bit of my experience and that of my companions when I say that he, who has experienced the magic of prayer, may do without food for days together, but not a single moment without prayer. For, without prayer there is no inward peace.

If that is the case, someone will say, we should be offering our prayers every minute of our lives. There is no doubt about it; but we, erring mortals, who find it difficult to retire within ourselves for inward communion even for a single moment, will find it impossible to remain perpetually in communion with the Divine. We, therefore, fix some hours when we make a serious effort to throw off the attach-ments of the world for a while, we make a serious endeavour to remain, so to say, out of the flesh. You have heard Surdas' hymn.* It is the passionate cry of a soul, hungering for union with the Divine. According to our standards, he was a saint ; but, according to his own, he was a proclaimed sinner. Spiritually, he was miles ahead of us; but he felt the separation from the Divine so keenly that he has uttered that anguished cry in loathing and despair.

I have talked of the necessity for prayer, and there-through I have dealt with the essence of prayer. We are born to serve our fellowmen, and we cannot properly do so unless we are wide awake. There is an eternal struggle raging in man's breast between the powers of darkness and of light, and he, who has not the sheet-anchor of prayer to

---

* 'Where is there a wretch
    So loathsome and wicked as I ?
I have forsaken my Maker,
    So faithless have I been.'

rely upon, will be a victim to the powers of darkness. The man of prayer will be at peace with himself and with the whole world; the man who goes about the affairs of the world without a prayerful heart, will be miserable and will make the world also miserable. Apart, therefore, from its bearing on man's condition after death, prayer has incalculable value for man in this world of the living. Prayer is the only means of bringing about orderliness and peace and repose in our daily acts. Take care of the vital thing and other things will take care of themselves. Rectify one angle of square, and the other angles will be automatically right.

Begin, therefore, your day with prayer, and make it so soulful that it may remain with you until the evening. Close the day with prayer so that you may have a peaceful night free from dreams and nightmares. Do not worry about the form of prayer. Let it be any form, it should be such as can put us into communion with the Divine. Only, whatever be the form, let not the spirit wander while the words of prayer run on out of your mouth.

Restraint self-imposed is no compulsion. A man who chooses the path of freedom from restraint, i.e., of self-indulgence, will be a bond slave of passions; whilst the man who binds himself to rules and restraints releases himself. All things in the universe, including the sun and the moon and the stars, obey certain laws. Without the restraining influence of these laws, the world would not go on for a single moment. You will go to pieces if you do not impose on yourselves some sort of discipline, and prayer is a necessary spiritual discipline. It is discipline and restraint that separates us from the brute. If we will be men, walking with our heads erect and not walking on all fours, let us understand and put ourselves under voluntary discipline and restraint.[8]

The Eternal Duel

MAN'S destined purpose is to conquer old habits, to overcome the evil in him and to restore good to its rightful place. If religion does not teach us how to achieve this conquest, it teaches us nothing. But there is no royal road to success in this the truest enterprise in life. Cowardice is, perhaps, the greatest vice from which we suffer and is also possibly the greatest violence, certainly far greater than bloodshed and the like that generally go under the name of violence. For, it comes from want of faith in God and ignorance of His attributes. I can give my own testimony and say that a heartfelt prayer is undoubtedly the most potent instrument that man possesses for overcoming cowardice and all other bad old habits. Prayer is an impossibility without a living faith in the presence of God within.

Christianity and Islam describe the same process as a duel between God and Satan, not outside but within; Zoroastrianism as a duel between Ahurmazd and Ahriman; Hinduism as a duel between forces of good and forces of evil. And to pray to God is nothing but that sacred alliance between God and man, whereby he attains his deliverance from the clutches of the Prince of Darkness.

But a heart-felt prayer is not a recitation with the lips. It is a yearning from within which expresses itself in every word, every act, nay, every thought of man. When an evil thought successfully assails him, he may know that he has offered but a lip prayer, and, similarly; with regard to an evil word escaping his lips or an evil act done by him. Real prayer is an absolute shield and protection against this trinity of evils. Success does not always attend the very first effort at such real living prayer. We have to strive against ourselves, we have to believe in spite of ourselves, because months are as our years. We have, therefore, to cultivate illimitable patience if we will realize the efficacy of prayer. There will be darkness, disappointment and even worse; but we must have courage enough to battle against all these and not succumb to cowardice. There is no such thing as retreat for a man of prayer.

What I am relating is not a fairy tale. I have not drawn an imaginary picture. I have summed up the testimony of men who have by prayer conquered every difficulty in their upward progress, and I have added my own humble testimony that the more I live the more I realize how much I owe to faith and prayer, which is one and the same thing for me. And I am quoting an experience not limited to a few hours, or days or weeks, but extending over an unbroken period of nearly 40 years. I have had my share of disappointments, uttermost darkness, counsels of despair, counsels of caution, subtlest assaults of pride; but I am able to say that my faith,—and I know that it is still little enough, by no means as great as I want it to be,—has ultimately conquered every one of these difficulties up to now.

If we have faith in us, if we have a prayerful heart, we may not tempt God, may not make terms with Him. We must reduce ourselves to a cipher. Not until we have reduced ourselves to nothingness, can we conquer the evil in us. God demands nothing less than complete self-surrender as the price for the only real freedom that is worth having. And when a man thus loses himself, he immediately finds himself in the service of all that lives. It becomes his delight and his recreation. He is a new man, never weary of spending himself in the service of God's creation.[9]

What is Faith ?

IT is faith that steers us through stormy seas, faith that moves mountains and faith that jumps across the ocean. That faith is nothing but a living, wide-awake consciousness of God within. He who has achieved that faith wants nothing.[10]

It is poor faith that needs fair weather for standing firm. That alone is true faith that stands the foulest weather.[11]

That faith is of little value which can flourish only in fair weather. Faith, in order to be of any value, has to survive the severest trials. Your faith is a whited sepulchre, if it cannot stand against the calumny of the whole world.[12]

Work without faith is like an attempt to reach the bottom of a bottomless pit.[13]

Faith can be turned into knowledge by experience, and it can come only through the heart and not by the intellect. The intellect, if anything, acts as a barrier in matters of faith.[14]

Limitations of Reason

EXPERIENCE has humbled me enough to let me realize the specific limitations of reason. Just as matter misplaced becomes dirt, reason misused becomes lunacy. If we would but render unto Caesar that which is Caesar's, all would be well.

Rationalists are admirable beings, rationalism is a hideous monster when it claims for itself omnipotence. Attribution of omnipotence to reason is as bad a piece of idolatry, as is worship of stock and stone believing it to be God.

Who has reasoned out the use of prayer? Its use is felt after practice. Such is the world's testimony. Cardinal Newman never surrendered his reason, but he yielded a better place to prayer, when he humbly sang: 'One step enough for me.' Shankara was a prince among reasoners. There is hardly anything in the world's literature to surpass Shankara's rationalism. But he yielded the first place to prayer and faith.

I do not know a single rationalist who has never done anything in simple faith and has based every one of his acts on reason. But we all know millions of human beings living their more or less orderly lives, because of their child-like faith in the Maker of us all. That very faith is a prayer.

The ancients did not delete from their lives the predominant function of faith and prayer. Works without faith and prayer are like an artificial flower that has no fragrance. I plead not for the suppression of reason, but for a due recognition of that in us which sanctifies reason itself.[15]

Faith Transcends Reason

Q. What counsel do you give to the young men who are fighting a losing battle with their lower selves and come to you for advice?

A. Simply prayer. One must humble oneself utterly, and look beyond oneself for strength.

Q. But what if the young men complain that their prayer is not heard, that they feel like speaking to brass heavens, as it were?

A. To want an answer to one's prayer is to tempt God. If prayer fails to bring relief, it is only lip-prayer. If prayer does not help, nothing else will. One must go on ceaselessly. This, then, is my message to the youth. In spite of themselves, the youth must believe in the all-conquering power of Love and Truth.

Q. The difficulty with our youth is that the study of science and modern philosophy has demolished their faith, and so they are burnt up by the fire of disbelief.

A. That is due to the fact that with them faith is an effort of the intellect, not an experience of the soul. Intellect takes us along in the battle of life to a certain limit, but at the crucial moment it fails us. Faith transcends reason. It is when the horizon is the darkest and human reason is beaten down to the ground, that faith shines brightest and comes to our rescue. It is such faith that our youth requires, and this comes when one has shed all pride of intellect and surrendered oneself entirely to His will.[16]

God Never Fails His Devotees

GOD never fails his devotees in the hour of trial. The condition is that there must be a living faith in and the uttermost reliance on Him. The test of faith is that having done our duty we must be prepared to welcome whatever He may send—joy as well as sorrow, good luck as well as bad. We will, then, feel like King Janaka who, when informed that his capital was ablaze, only remarked that it was no concern of his. The secret of his resignation and equanimity was that he was ever awake, never remiss in the performance of his duty. Having done his duty, he could leave the rest to God.

And so a man of prayer will, in the first place, be spared mishaps by the ever-merciful Providence; but if the mishaps do come, he will not bewail his fate but bear it with an undisturbed peace of mind and joyous resignation to His will.

Man is born to live in the midst of dangers and alarms. The whole existence of man is a ceaseless duel between the forces of life and death. God makes crooked straight for us, and sets things right when they seem to go dead wrong.[17]

' Beneath the Shadow of Thy Throne '

THE chief of the elephants had gone for a drink to the river, when he was caught hold of by an alligator. A furious struggle ensued, but, in spite of his strength, the elephant was dragged into deeper waters. When he was on the point of being drowned, the elephant realized that his huge strength was of no avail, and he prayed to God for succour. God, the Help of the helpless, came to his rescue and saved him from the jaws of death.

The moral is obvious. The strength of the strong without God's help has been often found to be useless. Therefore, I advise dependence not on outside sources but upon the inner strength which comes to all who sincerely seek it from God.

All human power is transient, and real safety can lie only when we place our reliance wholly on God.

"Beneath the shadow of Thy throne,
     Thy saints have dwelt serene;
Sufficient is Thine arm alone,
     And our defence is sure."

This is a lesson which all of us sorely need to learn.[18]

Faith in God

IF we have faith in God, we simply would not care to know beforehand how He may dispose of us. It is enough for us to hold ourselves perfectly in readiness for whatever happens. We are not allowed to know what tomorrow has in store for us, and our best conceived plans have a knack very often of going awry. The highest wisdom, therefore, is never to worry about the future, but to resign ourselves entirely to His Will.[19]

If we have trust in God, we should not worry even as we would not when we have a trustworthy door-keeper or guard. And who can be a better door-keeper or guard than God—the never-failing. It is not enough that we sing about such things or have a mere intellectual grasp. It is necessary to feel the thing within. Feeling is exactly like feeling pain or pleasure. It admits of or needs no argument. Who can argue us out of our experience?

Feeling is of the heart. It may easily lead us astray unless we would keep the heart pure. It is like keeping house and everything in it clean. The heart is the source from which knowledge of God springs. If the source is contaminated, every other remedy is useless. And if its purity is assured, nothing else is needed.[20]

Surrender to God's Will

YOU must not work yourself into anxiety. If we simply make ourselves instruments of His will, we should never have anxious moment.

Yes, there is no calm without a storm, there is no peace without strife. Strife is inherent in peace. We should not know it without. Life is a perpetual struggle against strife, whether within or without. Hence, the necessity of realizing peace in the midst of strife.[21]

We do not know God's hidden ways. If we only submit to Him, He makes us do many things even unconsciously to ourselves. It will be such a joy to me if you never find yourself in the Valley of Despair, for, to be there, even for one moment, means lack of faith in a living God.[22]

We are all in God's hands. Not a blade moves but by His command. If we had all our own ways, the world will go to pieces. It is perhaps as well that our wishes are often frustrated. It is the test of our loyalty to God that we believe in Him, even when He refuses to fulfil our wishes. I want you, therefore, to enjoy perfect peace even while things seem to you to be all going wrong.[23]

God does not always allow us to do what we think is the best. I suppose we don't always know what is best.[24]

The spirit of resignation is bad when the sorrows come out of our conscious errors; but when they come for reasons we do not know and cannot know, resignation is the proper thing. In other words, constant endeavour and surrender to the will of God have to go hand in hand.[25]

Whatever the ultimate issue, you must not be anxious about anything. Remember that God takes the burden of all our cares on His broad shoulders, if we will but let Him. This is as true as it is true that I am writing to you. Only His way is not our way, His shoulders are not like ours. But there is all the beauty in doing His will.[26]

' Be Careful for Nothing '

'BE careful for nothing' is one of the verses that have ever remained with me and taken possession of me. If God is, why need I care ? He is the infallible care-taker. He is a foolish man who fusses, although he is well protected.[27]

One who has any faith in God should be ashamed to worry about anything whatsoever. It is a difficult rule no doubt, for the simple reason that faith in God with the majority of mankind is either an intellectual belief or a blind belief, a kind of superstitious fear of something indefinable. But to ensure absolute freedom from worry requires a living utter faith which is a plant of slow, almost unperceived, growth and requires to be constantly watered by tears that accompany genuine prayer. They are the tears of a lover who cannot brook a moment's separation from the loved one, or of the penitent who knows that it is some trace of impurity in him that keeps him away from the loved one.[28]

The Test of Faith

DO we get all we want? If we did, where would our faith have any play at all? Sufficient to know that not a blade moves but by His will. He will take care, if we will but trust Him, not after the manner of those who will take all the care that money can procure and then trust. That we must take some care is true. But men of trust will not do violence to their own nature, and go out of their way to take precautions and adopt remedies which ordinary men have no means to command. The formula, therefore, is the less care the better, and no more than the least of us can procure by reasonable effort.[29]

It is a wrong thing to rehearse a calamity (i.e., an event believed by us to be calamity, though, in fact, it may be a blessing) and to reproduce in advance the feelings one would have. It is enough that we hold ourselves prepared for the worst. This we do by an ever increasing faith in God the Good, the Just, the Compassionate, the Bountiful, the Giver of the daily bread, the Help of the helpless, the All-Powerful, the All-Knowing, the Ever-Vigilant, the Whole Truth.[30]

Never imagine things good or bad, until they stare you in the face. Full surrender means full freedom from all care. A child never has care for anything. It knows instinctively that it is being cared for by its parents. How much more true should it be with us grown-up people? There you have the test of faith or detachment of the **Gita,** if you like.[31]

It is not faith that calculates, that fears, that hesitates. When a child nestles itself in the bosom of its mother and feels itself absolutely secure, it does not ask itself whether the mother is strong enough to protect it or not.[32]

Never imagine the worst. Since God is a God of Mercy, if we must imagine it is best to imagine the best. Of course, a votary of the **Gita** never imagines anything. Good and bad are after all relative terms. He takes note of things as they happen and reacts naturally to them, fulfilling his part as if propelled by the Great Mechanic, even as a piece of machine in good order responds automatically to the call of the mechanist. It is the most difficult thing for an intelligent being to be like a machine. And yet, if one is to become a zero, that is precisely what one desiring perfection has to become. The vital difference between the machine and the man is that the machine is inert, the man is all life and consciously becomes like a machine in the hands of the Master Mechanic. Krishna says, in so many words, that God moves all beings as if they were parts of a machine.[33]

If you have a living faith in a living God, you would feel His never-failing presence protecting you. Till that state is reached, even faith in an individual clothed in flesh and bone is not of any avail. It is relying on a broken reed. You should first think that out clearly, and then get the heart to co-operate with the intellect.[34]

You ought to learn real self-control. It does not come by reading. It comes only by definite realization that God is with us and looks after us as if He had no other care besides. How this happens, I do not know. That it does happen, I do know. Those who have faith, have all their cares lifted from off their shoulders. You cannot have faith and tension at the same time. Do relax your mind.[35]

But self-control to be self-control must brace one up. It becomes mechanical or superimposed when it unnerves or saddens one.[36]

There is something radically wrong in your carrying this load of anxiety on your shoulders. It is incompatible with a living faith in a living God. As days pass, I feel this Living Presence in every fibre of my veins. Without that feeling, I should be demented. There are so many things that are calculated to disturb my peace of mind. So many events happen that would, without the realization of that Presence, shake me to the very foundation. But they pass me by, leaving me practically untouched. I want you to share that reality with me.[37]

We have to acquire the faculty of keeping well under all weathers—a difficult task I know. But it is not beyond human reach. The mind plays a great part in it. If we can completely detach ourselves from the externals in terms of the Sixth Chapter, we can attain that state. That it appears to be beyond our reach for the present, need not baffle us. The author of the **Gita** invites us to the effort and says from his abundant experience that it never fails. It may take long, but success is a certainty.[38]

'Seek Ye First the Kingdom of God'

YOU say our fears are not due to want of faith in God, but want of faith in self. But these are one and the same thing. Want of faith in self comes from want of faith in God. It betrays ignorance of what God is. Then again, you say want of faith comes from our want of self-restraint. This is true, but it connotes the same thing. Read the verse 59 of Ch. II, **Gita**. Objects of senses are eradicated only by seeing God face to face; in other words, by faith in God. To have complete faith in God is to see Him. Nor is the matter any better by assuming the existence of the fourth dimension. It ultimately points to the same thing. 'Seek ye first the Kingdom of God and all else will be added unto you.' When we meet Him, we will dance in the joy of His Presence and there will be neither fear of snakes, nor of the death of dear ones. For, there is no death and no snake-bite in His Presence. The fact is that the most living faith, too, falls short of the perfect. Hence, there is no such thing

as complete absence of fear for the embodied, **i.e.,** impri-
soned soul. The possession of the body is a limitation. It
is a wall of separation. We can, therefore, but try to shed
our fear **i.e.,** increase our faith.[39]

SOURCES

AO : ASHRAM OBSERVANCES, *by* M. K. Gandhi. Navajivan Karyalaya, Ahmedabad.

AS : TO ASHRAM SISTERS, *by* M. K. Gandhi. Navajivan Karyalaya, Ahmedabad.

BLM : BAPU'S LETTERS TO MIRA, *by* M. K. Gandhi. Navajivan Karyalaya, Ahmedabad.

DD : DELHI DIARY, *by* M. K. Gandhi. Navajivan Karyalaya, Ahmedabad.

DMD : DIARY OF MAHADEV DESAI, *by* Mahadev Desai. Navajivan Karyalaya, Ahmedabad.

ER : ETHICAL RELIGION, *by* M. K. Gandhi. S. Ganesan, Madras.

H : HARIJAN, a weekly journal edited *by* M. K. Gandhi.

HS : HIND SWARAJ, *by* M. K. Gandhi. Navajivan Karyalaya, Ahmedabad.

HT : HINDUSTAN TIMES, daily newspaper published in New Delhi.

ICS : INDIA'S CASE FOR SWARAJ, *by* M. K. Gandhi. Yeshanand & Co., Bombay.

MDC : MY DEAR CHILD, *by* M. K. Gandhi. Navajivan Karyalaya, Ahmedabad.

ML : MEANING OF LIFE, *by* Will Durant. Published by Williams & Norgates Ltd., London.

SL : SELECTED LETTERS, *by* M. K. Gandhi. Navajivan Karyalaya, Ahmedabad.

SSA : SATYAGRAHA IN SOUTH AFRICA, *by* M. K. Gandhi. Navajivan Karyalaya, Ahmedabad.

SW : SPEECHES AND WRITINGS OF MAHATMA GANDHI. G. A. Natesan, Madras.

YI : YOUNG INDIA, a weekly journal edited *by* M. K. Gandhi.

YM : FROM YERAVDA MANDIR, *by* M. K. Gandhi. Navajivan Karyalaya, Ahmedabad.

UTL : UNTO THIS LAST—A Paraphrase *by* M. K. Gandhi. Navajivan Karyalaya, Ahmedabad.

REFERENCES

CHAPTER I

1. UTL, ix
2. ER, 34-59.

CHAPTER II

1. SW, 350.
2. YI, March 17, 1927.
3. YM, Chap. VI.
4. YI, April 30. 1931.
5. H, Feb. 1, 1942.
6. HS, 32.
7. H, Aug. 29, 1936.
8. H, Sept. 1, 1946.
9. H, July 21, 1946.

CHAPTER III

1. YI, Oct. 7, 1926.
2. H, Oct. 6, 1946.
3. YI, Nov. 26, 1931.
4. H, March 31, 1946.
5. YI, Sept. 4, 1930.
6. AS, 105.
7. MDC, 17.
8. YI, Feb. 5, 1925.
9. H, Feb. 1, 1942.
10. H, Feb. 22, 1942.
11. H, March 8, 1942.
12. YI, Oct. 6, 1927.
13. H, Feb. 23, 1947.
14. H, July 28, 1940.
15. DMD, 155.

CHAPTER IV

1. H, June 29, 1935.
2. H, March 2, 1947.
3. H, Sept. 8. 1946.
4. H, Feb. 23, 1947.
5. H, Feb. 8, 1939.

CHAPTER V

1. YI, Oct. 10, 1929.
2. YI, Jan. 17, 1926.

3. YI, Feb. 28, 1929.
4. YI, Nov. 14, 1929.
5. YI, April 30, 1925.
6. YI, Jan. 6, 1927.
7. YI, April 29, 1926.

CHAPTER VI

1. YI, May, 13, 1926.
2. YI, March 21, 1929.
3. YI, April 25, 1929.
4. H, March 31, 1946.
5. YI, March 12, 1931.

CHAPTER VII

1. YI, Oct. 25, 1928.
2. BLM, 128.
3. BLM, 142.
4. BLM, 139.
5. BLM, 124.
6. H, Sept. 24, 1938.

CHAPTER VIII

1. YI, Jan. 8, 1925.
2. YI, Jan. 15, 1925.
3. YI, Oct. 4, 1928.
4. H, May 26, 1946.
5. DMD, 285, 293.
6. YI, Oct. 11, 1928.
7. YI, Nov. 1, 1928.
8. YI, Aug. 29, 1929.
9. H, March 18, 1939.
10. H, Oct. 14, 1939.
11. H, May 27, 1939.
12. H, June 8, 1947.
13. YI, Oct. 10, 1929.
14. H, July 6, 1947.
15. H, Nov. 30, 1947.
16. H, Aug. 17, 1947.

CHAPTER IX

1. H, July 13, 1947.
2. HS, 39.
3. YI, July 17, 1924.

4. H, Aug. 18, 1940.
5. SSA, 480.
6. YI, Dec. 26, 1924.
7. H, Sept. 22, 1940.
8. H, April 20, 1947.
9. YI, Aug. 14, 1924.

CHAPTER X

1. H, May 4, 1935.
2. H, March 13, 1937.
3. H, May 28, 1938.
4. H, April 2, 1938.
5. H, May 8, 1937.
6. H, July 28, 1946.
7. DMD, 175.
8. H, June 2, 1946.
9. DMD, 250.

CHAPTER XI

1. ML, 13.
2. H, Aug. 29, 1936.
3. DMD, 184.
4. YI, Oct. 20, 1927.
5. YI, Oct. 27, 1927.
6. H, April 6, 1947.
7. H, Oct. 13, 1946.
8. H, Nov. 10, 1946.
9. YI, Feb. 14, 1929.
10. H, July 21, 1946.
11. AS, 80.
12. H, May 19, 1946.
13. H, Oct. 20, 1946.
14. AS, 3.
15. AS, 14, 46.
16. SL, 25.
17. DMD, 296.
18. SL, 22.
19. SL, 23.
20. H, Feb. 2, 1947.
21. AO, 67.
22. YM, Chap. XVI.
23. H, March 23, 1947.
24. DMD, 287.
25. H, Sept. 8, 1946.
26. YI, Sept. 8, 1927.
27. YM, Chap. XIV.
28. YM, Chap. XV.

CHAPTER XII

1. YI, Jan. 10, 1929.
2. H, Jan. 26, 1947.
3. H, April 6, 1940.
4. H, Sept. 15, 1940.
5. H, Dec. 12, 1936.
6. YI, Feb. 16, 1922.
7. H, Dec. 8, 1946.
8. H, May 27, 1939.
9. AS, 72.
10. DMD, 177.
11. H, April 7, 1946.
12. H, Jan. 16, 1937.
13. H, Feb. 6, 1937.
14. H, Oct. 20, 1946.
15. YI, Jan. 3, 1929.
16. YI, Sept 10, 1925.

CHAPTER XIII

1. YM, Chap. XII.
2. AS, 53.
3. YI, Jan. 12, 1928.
4. SL, 44.
5. DMD, 263.
6. YI, Jan. 12, 1928.
7. YI, June 25, 1925.
8. YM, Chap. XII.

CHAPTER XIV

1. H, Feb. 2, 1934.
2. DMD, 276.
3. YI, Oct. 13, 1921.
4. DMD, 20.
5. YI, Jan. 21, 1926.
6. YI, Oct. 11, 1928.
7. SSA, 286.
8. YI, May 21, 1923.
9. YI, Dec. 13, 1928.
10. H, Feb. 22, 1948.
11. ICS, 245.
12. YI, Dec. 30, 1926.
13. YI, Jan. 13, 1927.
14. YI, March 12, 1930.
15. YI, Oct. 13, 1921.
16. YI, Feb. 7, 1929.
17. YI, Sept. 12, 1929.
18. H, July 28, 1946.
19. H, Sept. 19, 1936.

20. H, Aug. 18, 1946.
21. YI, Feb. 2, 1942.
22. DD, 6.
23. H, June 23, 1946.
24. H, Nov. 30, 1947.
25. H, July 6, 1940.
26. H, Oct. 6, 1946.
27. YI, April 14, 1927.
28. H, April 20, 1947.
29. H, Jan. 25, 1948.
30. SL, 18, 24, 34.
31. AS, 68.
32. YI, Nov. 20, 1924.
33. SL, 18.
34. YI, May 12, 1927.
35. YI, April 21, 1927.
36. YI, Sept. 23, 1925.
37. YI, Oct. 25, 1928.
38. BLM, 12.
39. BLM, 41.
40. BLM, 154.
41. BLM, 156.
42. BLM, 159.
43. BLM, 194.
44. BLM, 196.
45. BLM, 260.
46. BLM, 301.
47. BLM, 323.
48. DMD, 254-55.
49. H, Feb. 15, 1948.
50. DMD, 118.
51. DMD, 146.
52. H, Aug. 19, 1939.
53. H, June 1, 1940.

15. YI, Oct. 14, 1926.
16. YI, March 21, 1929.
17. H, July 7, 1946.
18. H, Jan. 5, 1947.
19. H, May 12, 1946.
20. MDC, 89-91.
21. MDC, 90.
22. MDC, 99.
23. MDC, 102.
24. MDC, 113.
25. MDC, 110.
26. MDC, 112.
27. DMD, 149.
28. YI, Sept. 1, 1927.
29. BLM, 67.
30. BLM, 233.
31. BLM, 235.
32. YI, Dec. 15, 1927.
33. BLM, 238.
34. BLM, 280.
35. BLM, 267.
36. BLM, 170.
37. BLM, 268.
38. BLM, 272.
39. BLM, 231.

CHAPTER XV

1. YI, Jan. 23, 1930.
2. HT, Feb. 7, 1946.
3. H, April 14, 1946.
4. H, June 22, 1935.
5. YI, Sept. 25, 1924.
6. SL, 5.
7. YI, March 31, 1920.
8. YI, Jan. 23, 1930.
9. YI, Dec. 20, 1928.
10. YI, Sept. 24, 1925.
11. YI, Nov. 20, 1924.
12. YI, April 25, 1929.
13. H, Oct. 30, 1936.
14. H, June 18, 1938.